LEWIS AND CLARK EXPLORATION OF CENTRAL MONTANA

MARIAS RIVER TO THE GATES OF THE MOUNTAINS

by Ella Mae Howard

Illustrations by Tom English and Robert Moritz
Maps by Robert Bergantino
Cover by Robert Orduno

Lewis and Clark Interpretative Association, Inc.
Great Falls, Montana

Lewis And Clark On Their Historic Expedition To The Pacific Coast Discovered This Giant Fountain On June 18, 1805. In Honor Of The Courage, Fidelity And Patriotism Of The Explorers This Tablet Is Here Placed And Dedicated By The Black Eagle Chapter, Daughters Of The American Revolution, May 30, 1928.

—marble marker located just above Giant Springs

Published by the Lewis and Clark Interpretative Association, Inc.
P.O. Box 2848
Great Falls, Montana 59403

Library of Congress Catalog Card Number 93-78883

ISBN: 1-883844-03-7

6th Printing, July 2000

TABLE OF CONTENTS

LIST OF MAPS

Acknowledgements

Lewis and Clark Exploration of Central Montana is the fulfillment of a promise made to the Lewis and Clark Interpretative Association of Great Falls. Thanks to the Association, I had the opportunity to put together this work on two of my favorite people, Lewis and Clark.

Several people helped with this book and I appreciate their efforts. Tom English and Robert Moritz donated their artistic talents to add flavor to the text. Robert Orduno, an artist of Santa Fe, New Mexico, allowed us to use a portion of his Great Falls International Airport mural for the cover. Joyce Ziegenhagel volunteered to type the first draft from my notes; this was no easy task.

Jeri Pullum, manuscript reviewer, had the patience to work with me through all of the revisions and I appreciate that. Ken Walcheck and Bob Doerk offered suggestions, many of which I gratefully used.

To Robert Bergantino of Butte, Montana, I offer a very appreciative acknowledgement for the maps and for his critical review of the text. Mr. Bergantino read the text with a keen eye for accuracy. His suggestions made this a better book than I could have written without his help. Thank you Bob.

With this edition, the book has been expanded to fill several gaps that existed in the previous edition. Hopefully, it is now more enlightening on the Lewis and Clark Expedition in central Montana.

— *Ella Mae Howard*

INTRODUCTION

This book looks at the Lewis and Clark Expedition in central Montana between the Marias River and the Gates of the Mountains, west to the Continental Divide. Although this is a relatively small part of the area explored by Lewis and Clark, the time they spent here is rich in discoveries and happenings.

Late in the afternoon of June 2, 1805, in what is today north central Montana, the Lewis and Clark Expedition arrived at the confluence of the Marias and Missouri Rivers. Lewis described the north fork as "a very considerable river." There was no small amount of confusion as the Captains tried to decide which of the two rivers was the true Missouri.

The dilemma at the Marias was the first time the men faced a decision on which the fate of the Expedition rested. And, just a few days after successfully wrestling with the problem at the Marias, Lewis and Clark faced the equally difficult problem of portaging their canoes and equipment eighteen miles around the falls of the Missouri.

In the summer of 1806, Lewis and nineteen members of the Expedition came back through this same area. Lewis, while exploring the upper Marias River drainage, experienced the only armed conflict of the Expedition. During this confrontation, at least one Indian was killed with another left wounded.

President Thomas Jefferson, who once wrote: "It is truly remarkable that so few public figures take notes, without which history becomes fable instead of fact," instructed Expedition members to keep detailed journals of what they saw and did. In addition to the two Captains, Joseph Whitehouse, John Ordway and Charles Floyd kept journals that are extant in their original form. Patrick Gass' journal was first published in 1807 in a paraphrased edition written by David McKeehan. The original Gass journal does not exist today. Lewis indicated that the sergeants were keeping journals, so it is assumed there was a Nathaniel Pryor journal; it, however, has never been found. Within a couple of months of the Expedition's return to St. Louis, a prospectus indicating Robert Frazier's intentions to publish his journal appeared in newspapers. The Frazier journal, however, never appeared in print. The Frazier prospectus is preserved in the Wisconsin Historical Society and there is a map related to the Frazier journal in the Library of Congress. The entries of the six known journalists provide a fascinating picture of Expedition activities in this area and give us descriptions of what the land was like before permanent settlement came to be.

These journals are the primary source of information for this book. All quotations are from the Moulton edition of the journals unless otherwise indicated. To give the reader a more direct sense of the feelings and thoughts of the Expedition members as they pushed on every day toward the west and then, in 1806 as their thoughts and efforts returned them to the east and their homes, this work contains many of the words and sentences they wrote as quotations from their daily journals.

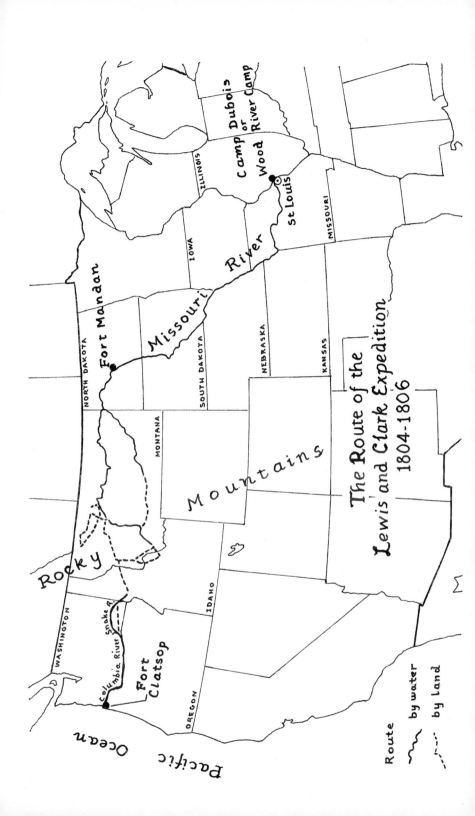

The Route of the
Lewis and Clark Expedition
1804-1806

Camp Dubois
or
Wood River Camp

St Louis

ILLINOIS

MISSOURI

IOWA

Missouri River

Fort Mandan

NORTH DAKOTA

SOUTH DAKOTA

NEBRASKA

KANSAS

MONTANA

Mountains

Rocky

IDAHO

WASHINGTON

Snake R.

Columbia River

Fort Clatsop

OREGON

Pacific Ocean

Route
⌇ by water
--- by land

THE EXPEDITION

On January 18, 1803, President Thomas Jefferson asked the Congress of the United States for $2,500 to send an expedition to explore the west. The request was approved and a year later, Jefferson's dream of sending a small group of men to explore the Missouri River to its source and continue to the Pacific Ocean became a reality. Jefferson and the men who voted approval of the idea hoped to find the fabled Northwest Passage, the water route across the wide expanses of an uncharted continent. Although this was the primary goal, Jefferson as a man with an unquenchable thirst for knowledge, particularly knowledge of natural things, also wanted to know about the plant and animal life, the Indians, the weather, the landscape, anything in nature new to the American scientific community. Jefferson's letter of instructions dated June 20, 1803 gave Meriwether Lewis a simple, but comprehensive list of what the President expected from the exploration.

The Expedition spent the winter of 1803-1804 at the mouth of the Wood River near St. Louis, Missouri preparing for the journey. It was during this time that the more often rowdy, robustious recruits were taught the importance of discipline and following orders. In the spring, the Captains learned that the international right to lay claim on at least part of the country to be explored had been purchased by the United States from France. (This claim was recognized by other nations. It was then up to the United States to buy it, win it or whatever from the actual inhabitants.) This placed an additional burden on the Captains because now the Indians they were sure to meet along the Missouri River and its tributaries were the newest citizens of the United States and the Captains would have the duty to explain what this might mean to the Indians.

On May 14, 1804, the Corps of Discovery under the command of Captains Meriwether Lewis and William Clark departed its winter encampment and started up the muddy spring-runoff waters of the Missouri. The party was much larger than the 10-12 men Jefferson had suggested. Nearly fifty men were in two pirogues and a keelboat, and two men were riding horses. On a good day, the men would manage twenty-five miles. Other days it was ten to fifteen miles. The Expedition spent the summer tracing the Missouri River to the Mandan Indian territory in central North Dakota. The winter of 1804-1805 was endured in a fort the men constructed on the north bank of the Missouri River near the Indian villages.

After surviving a bitterly cold winter on the high plains during which the temperature frequently fell many degrees below zero, the party of thirty-three which included the new recruits Toussaint Charbonneau, Sacagawea, two-month old Jean Baptiste Charbonneau and John Baptiste Lepage departed on April 7, 1805. Traveling in six cottonwood dugout canoes the men had hollowed out during the spring and with the two pirogues, the Expedition crossed the 104th parallel into what is now Montana. It was April 27, just twenty days after Lewis wrote the words:

> "we were now about to penetrate a country at least two thousand miles in width, on which the foot of civillized man had never trodden; the good or evil it had in store for us was for experiment yet to determine, and these little vessells contained every article by which we were to ex-pect to subsist or defend ourselves. however as this the state of mind in which we are, generally gives the colouring to events, when the immagination is suffered to wander into futurity, the picture which now presented itself to me was a most pleasing one."

The rest of the summer into mid-August, the Lewis and Clark party pulled, paddled and poled the canoes to the headwaters of the Missouri, and then with the help of horses obtained from the Shoshoni Indians entered the Bitterroot Mountains near Missoula, Montana. From there, the party after struggling across the Lolo Trail, followed the Clearwater, Snake and Columbia Rivers to the Pacific Ocean.

The winter of 1805-1806 was spent at a fort constructed roughly three miles south of present-day Astoria, Oregon on the west bank of a stream now called the Lewis and Clark River. This is about one and a half miles south of the south shore of Youngs Bay. Fort Clatsop, named in honor of the Clatsop Indians, was home for the party until March 23, 1806 when the Expedition started its return journey.

By July 3, 1806, the Expedition had returned to the eastern slopes of the Bitterroot Mountains. Here the party separated. Captain Clark would explore the Yellowstone River; Captain Lewis would follow the Blackfoot River to Lewis and Clark Pass and then proceed to the Great Falls area from the Sun River. Sergeant Ordway with Clark's party would return to Camp Fortunate, raise the canoes, then return to the three forks. From there Clark would explore the Yellowstone, while Sergeant Ordway and nine Expedition members would continue to the great falls.

Forty days after their separation, the two captains were reunited August 12 on the Missouri River in North Dakota. After a brief stop near Fort Mandan, the Expedition continued down the Missouri arriving in St. Louis on September 23, 1806. The epic journey lasted more than two years (two years, four months, nine days) and covered 8,000 miles.

WHICH RIVER TO FOLLOW

Lewis and Clark were fifty-six days out of Fort Mandan when, in north central Montana, they arrived at the confluence of the Marias and Missouri Rivers. To this point, they had followed the Missouri across the vast reaches of the northern plains, through the beautiful scenery of the White Cliffs, and emerged to view what Lewis described as "rich level and extensive plains on both sides of the river."

On June 3, 1805, after recognizing the seriousness of the problem, Lewis wrote, "An interesting question was now to be determined; which of these rivers was the Missouri....to mistake the stream at this period of the season, two months of the traveling season having now elapsed, and to ascend such stream to the rocky Mountain or perhaps much further before we could inform ourselves whether it did approach the Columbia or not, and then be obliged to return and take the other stream would not only loose us the whole of this season but would probably so dishearten the party that it might defeat the expedition altogether." In the next few days, Lewis and Clark struggled with making a decision on which the future of the Expedition rested.

Unlike the other major tributaries the Expedition had come across, the Marias was totally unexpected. No such river had been included in the geography lesson the Indians had given them during the previous winter and spring. Before Lewis closed out his journal on June 3, he expressed his irritation: "what astonishes us a little is that the Indians who appeared to be so well acquainted with the geography of this country should not have mentioned this river....I am equally astonished at their not mentioning the S. fork which they must have passed in order to

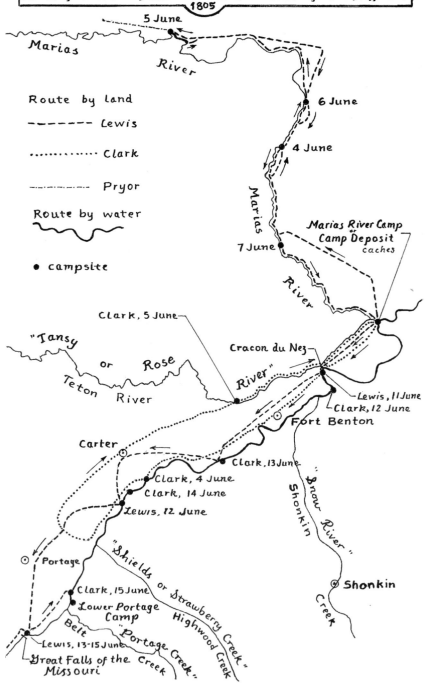

The Route and Campsites of the Lewis and Clark Expedition —
Mouth of the Marias River to the Great Falls of the Missouri
1805

5 June

Marias   River

Route by land

------- Lewis

············· Clark

----·---- Pryor

Route by water

● campsite

6 June

4 June

Marias

Marias River Camp
or
Camp Deposit
caches

7 June

River

Clark, 5 June

"Tansy   or   Rose

Teton   River

River"

Cracon du Nez

Lewis, 11 June
Clark, 12 June

Fort Benton

Carter

Clark, 13 June

Clark, 4 June
Clark, 14 June

Lewis, 12 June

Shonkin   "Snow River"

Creek

Shonkin

⊙ Portage

Clark, 15 June

Lower Portage
Camp

"Shields or Strawbery   Highwood Creek

Belt   "Portage   Creek"

Lewis, 13-15 June

Great Falls of the   Creek
Missouri

get to those large falls which they mention on the Missouri. thus have our cogitating faculties been busily employed all day."

It is understandable that Lewis, in June 1805, was upset because the Indians had not mentioned this river flowing into the Missouri. But today, there is a better concept of the relationships and travel of the different tribes. The Blackfeet Indians controlled the country north and west of the point where Lewis wrote his words in 1805. They were an aggressive tribe feared by other Indians including those with whom the Expedition had wintered. It therefore makes sense that the Indians from the Mandan country did not follow the Missouri to the western mountains, but went overland avoiding the country around the confluence of the two rivers particularly that to the north. Perhaps, the Indians of the Mandan country who pushed dirt into piles to represent mountains and scratched lines for rivers on the dirt chalk board failed to trace out this "considerable river" because they did not know about it.

In contrast to the Captains, the men of the Expedition welcomed the chance for a rest. The never-ceasing westerly winds and strong river current had taken their toll. Lewis wrote: "Those who have remained at camp today have been busily engaged in dressing skins for cloathing, notwithstanding that many of them have their feet so mangled and bruised with the stones and rough ground over which they passed barefoot, that they can scarcely walk or stand; at least it is with great pain they do either. for some days past they were unable to wear their mockersons...."

Ordway indicated the men had difficulty keeping their moccasins on owing to the "Stiffness of the mud & decline of the Steepp hill sides." On their arrival at the Marias, he wrote, "we to be Sure have a hard time of it oblidged to walk on Shore &

hawl the rope and 9/10 of their time barefooted." Through all of this though the men, according to Lewis, "remain perfectly cheerfull."

On June 3, the two Captains "stroled out to the top of the hights in the fork of these rivers" and on their return to camp had discovered "a handsome little river falling into the N. fork on Lard. side...." They called this little river Rose River (also Tansy, Tansey) because of "the wild rose which grows here in great abundance...now in full bloom, and adds not a little to the beaty of the cenery." Today Lewis' Rose River is called the Teton River, after Teton Butte located twelve miles west of Choteau which has the characteristic shape of a woman's breast.

The decision had to be made. Lewis wrote, "to this end an investigation of both streams was the first thing to be done...." Sergeant Gass and two others were sent up the south fork, while Sergeant Pryor and two men tackled the north fork. Both were to be back by nightfall with their reports. It was determined the north fork was not as wide as the south fork, but "it's waters run in the same boiling and roling maner...." The south fork on the other hand, "is perfectly transparent runds very rappid...." The reports of the two sergeants did not satisfy the Captains, and it was decided a more extensive investigation was needed before the party could choose which river led to the source of the Missouri River and the supposed low gap in the mountains.

On June 4, Lewis, Pryor, Drouillard, Shields, Windsor, Cruzatte and Lepage left on foot to explore the north fork. They were gone five days and traveled sixty miles to a point about eight miles downstream from the mouth of Pondera Coulee (twelve miles east of Tiber Dam). For their return, Lewis had two rafts built; however, as he wrote, "were soon convinced that this mode of navigation was hazerdous particularly with those rafts they being too small and slender." After nearly losing a gun and wetting their baggage, they abandoned the rafts and again took to walking the muddy plains above the river.

During most of the five days, cold June rain was the constant companion of Lewis and the six men. On June 6, the final words Lewis penned into his journal were "it continues to rain and we have no shelter, an uncomfortable nights rest is the natural consequence."

June 7 dawned with more rain and cold wind. By now, Lewis and his men had become well acquainted with the gumbo of central Montana. He wrote, "notwithstanding the rain that has now fallen the earth of these bluffs is not wet to a greater debth than 2 inches; in it's present state it is precisely like walking over frozan grownd which is thawed to small debth and slips equally as bad." Both Lewis and Windsor nearly slipped into the river from the steep bluffs lining the Marias in this area. Lewis with the aid of his espontoon (officer's pike) had just escaped his predicament of nearly plunging ninety feet down the clift to almost certain death when he heard Windsor cry out "god god Capt. what shall I do…" Windsor had slipped and was lying on his stomach with his right arm and leg over the cliff's edge. He managed to avoid sliding down the precipitous bank by holding onto the ground with his left arm and foot. Lewis wrote, "I expected every instant to see him loose his strength and slip off…." Lewis disguised his fear and calmly told Windsor to take his knife from his belt and with his right hand dig a hole in the face of the cliff into which he could place his right foot. The young man did as directed and was able to escape plunging down the bank. Lewis then directed the others who were following to work their way down to the edge of the river and pass the jagged break by wading the river at the foot of the cliff.

Clark, the two Field brothers, Gass, Shannon and York spent three days exploring the south fork. The first day of overland travel took Clark's party to the ridge which separates the Teton River from the Missouri River by what Clark estimated to be 100 yards. This narrow ridge was in later years called the *Cracon du Nez* (bridge of the nose) by French fur traders. Clark's party took a short respite at a spring that bubbled from the banks of the Missouri River as it washed the narrow ridge before sliding back toward the center of its valley. Most likely this spring was caused by water seeping under the *Cracon du Nez* from the Teton River channel which, at this point, is several feet higher in elevation than the channel of the Missouri River. Gass wrote in his journal that they stopped at the spring and enjoyed a drink of grog (rum and water). This moment of enjoyment resulted in the name "Grog Spring."

During the waning hours of June 4, Clark and his party made camp near the Missouri River. Two grizzly bears were in the area and one of them gave Joseph Field a turn on the grizzly bear carousel. From the vantage of those watching, it appeared Field was in a battle he might loose. His rifle was wet and would not fire, and the bear was so close to him the others could not fire for fear of hitting him. The bear and the young man got within arm's length of each other but the only evidence of the close encounter was a scratch on Field's leather-covered foot. Finally the bear was convinced to leave by the others' hollering and firing their rifles in the air.

Clark had not traveled far, about eleven miles, on the second day of his exploration of the south fork when he became convinced it was the true Missouri. He wasted little time in making his decision and started the return walk to the confluence of the two rivers. He wrote, "I could discover that the river run west of

South a long distance, and has a Strong rapid Current as this river Continued its width debth & rapidity and the Course west of South, going up further would be useless, I deturmined to return...."

Even though he had found no falls, Clark returned to camp at the confluence convinced he had made the correct decision. Likewise, Lewis returned with the idea that the north fork could not be the Missouri because it bore too far north and there were no falls on it. According to Whitehouse, a "Council" was held and the men were asked their opinion on which river to follow. The men were swayed by the lobbying efforts of Cruzatte and no amount of reasoning by the Captains could convince them the south fork was the Missouri River. They preferred to follow the gut feeling of Cruzatte. Whitehouse wrote, "our officers & all the men differ in their opinions which river to take." Lewis noted in this journal that Cruzatte, an experienced and respected waterman, "declared it as his opinion the N. fork was the true genuine Missouri and could be no other."

Visitors to the confluence of the two rivers today are often given to questioning why all the struggle with the decision of which river to follow. It seems so obvious. But our observations today are based on what is seen two hundred years after the fact, not what Lewis saw just after the turn of the 19th century. Perhaps the best explanation is based on the weather patterns and the remnants of a late 1700's cold period. There is no doubt the Expedition experienced a cold spring. Nighttime temperatures in late May and early June made ice in the water kettles and the mountains were white with snow. Water from the spring runoff in the plains reached the Marias River sooner than the water from the mountain snow pack reached the Missouri River. Maybe with the extraordinary cold weather of the spring of 1805, the mountains of the upper Missouri watershed had not given up much water by the time Lewis arrived at the confluence whereas the plains which feed runoff water to the Marias had warmed sufficiently to produce flood-like levels of water. Lewis and Clark's struggle at the Marias may have simply been caused by a matter of timing.

Understanding the gravity of the situation, Lewis and Clark agreed it was necessary to confirm that they had arrived at the correct decision, and the one way to do this was to find the falls which the Indians had told them were on the Missouri. So, it was agreed Lewis would take four men and proceed by land "untill we found the falls or reached the snowy Mountains...." Clark with the main party would proceed up the south fork until he heard from Lewis.

Once satisfied the north fork was not the Missouri, Lewis named it Maria's River for his Virginia cousin, Maria Wood. Over the years, the apostrophe has been dropped and the river that caused Lewis and Clark so much consternation is now known as the Marias. It is pronounced as if it were spelled Mariahs. Ordway, the most faithful journalist of the Lewis and Clark writers, had several phonetic spellings for the name of the river, "Moriah, Mariah, Morriahs, Marriahs," which showed his effort to spell the name as it sounded when Captain Lewis pronounced it.

The two Captains did not give their camp at the confluence a name. Ordway however called it "Camp on point Deposite which is 2508 1/4 miles from the Mouth of the Missourie." For those serious students of Lewis' Expedition, the camp at the mouth of the Marias was called Camp Deposit by two Lewis and Clark journalists, Ordway and Whitehouse. Whitehouse often copied Ordway's journal, so Ordway is usually given credit for the name "Camp Deposit."

During the ten-day stay at the mouth of the Marias, the Captains determined to lighten the load on the men by leaving the red pirogue and some of the baggage. Lewis wrote, "we drew up the red perogue into the middle of a small Island at the entrance of Maria's river, and secured and made her fast to the trees to prevent the high floods from carrying her off put my brand on several trees standing near her...." They also dug several caches in which a number of items were stored until the next year.

And, according to Whitehouse, during the evening of June 9 at the Marias River, "we had a frolick the officers gave the party a dram, the fiddle played and they danced late &c...."

BARN MOUNTAIN

On June 4 when Lewis reached a high point above the confluence of the Marias and Missouri Rivers on his exploration of the Marias, he wrote: "The Barn Mountain, a lofty mountain so called from it's resemblance to the roof of a large Barn, is a seperate Mountain and appears reather to the wright of and retreating from the extremity of the S. mts.; this boar S. 38 W. distant 35 ms." Standing on the same high point as Lewis did in 1805, no such mountain can be seen to the southwest. The view to the southeast, however, reveals Lewis' Barn Mountain, known today as Square Butte just east of the Highwood Mountains. The Captain apparently made a mistake when he recorded the bearings.

The Captains often climbed high points to take compass bearings or readings and report on what they saw from the lofty spots. From his vantage point above the Marias, Lewis could see the Rocky Mountains to the west, the Bears Paw Mountains (which he called the North Mountains) to the north and the Highwood Mountains (which he called the South Mountains) to the southeast. He could have also seen the Little Belt Mountains which during his 1806 ride up the Marias, he called the "falls mountains." On the walk up the Marias in 1805 and in 1806, as he rode horseback in the same area, he reported seeing lofty mountains to the northwest; the middle one of these three island mountains he called "Tower Mountain." Collectively, he called these rugged, craggy mountains the "broken Mountains." Today, these are the Sweet Grass Hills.

TO THE FALLS

Once the decision was made to proceed up the south fork, the Captains lost little time in laying their plans. Captain Clark and the main party would move upstream in the canoes and white pirogue. Lewis and his party of four (Drouillard, Joseph Field, Gibson, Goodrich) would go overland to look for the falls.

Although Lewis was "somewhat unwell with the disentary," he was determined to carry out his part of the plan and, accordingly, on June 11, departed the main camp. He lead his party along the strip of land between the Missouri and Teton Rivers until about noon when, after the "short march of 9 miles," the party crossed the *Cracon du Nez.* Here they saw a herd of elk on the Missouri River and shot four of the animals. The elk were butchered and the meat hung in the trees for Clark's party.

Before Lewis' men could prepare dinner, the Captain became very ill with a high fever and intestinal upsets, and was unable to enjoy the "feast of marrowbones." His illness prevented any more walking for the day, so he had a camp of willow boughs prepared and spent the rest of the day there. Lewis wrote, "having brought no medecine with me I resolved to try an experiment...." He had the men collect twigs from chokecherry bushes. After the leaves were removed, he boiled the twigs to make "a strong black decoction of an astringent bitter tast." Lewis drank one pint at sunset and followed with another about an hour later. He described the success of his experiment by writing that "by 10 in the evening I was entirely releived from pain...and I had a comfortable and refreshing nights rest."

The next morning, June 12, Lewis and his party set out at sunrise. Their route kept them about three miles from the river roughly parallel to it, but far enough away to avoid the deep coulee cuts feeding into the river. After traveling twelve miles, Lewis "boar a little to the south in order to gain the river as well to obtain water to allay my thirst as to kill something for breakfast; for the plain through which we had been passing possesses no water and is so level that we cannot approach the buffaloe within shot before they discover us and take to flight." Near the river, the party met "two large bear, and killed them boath at the first fire, a circumstance" Lewis wrote "never happend with the party in killing the brown bear before."

After eating what they wanted of bear meat for breakfast, they hung the rest of the meat and skins in the trees for Clark. By the time they had killed the bears which Lewis wrote was about 10 a.m. and had had the first food of the day, they had walked fifteen miles. They allowed themselves a couple of hours rest, then ascended the steep bluffs to start across the plain again in search of the falls. Lewis and his men continued their overland march until nearly dark, covering another twelve miles or so to "a handsome little bottom of Cottonwood timber" just upstream from present-day Black Coulee in Chouteau County.

Lewis understandably felt a little weary after marching twenty-seven miles, but it was his opinion the weariness was caused by the illness from the previous day, not the long walk. His appetite was much improved and he "ate very heartily." He spent the evening catching the "white fish" (sauger-*Stizostedion canadense*) and, before he allowed himself to sleep, he wrote a wonderful discussion on a species of tree, the narrowleaf cottonwood (*Populus angustifolia*), that was just beginning to make its appearance along the banks of the river.

Clark and the canoe party departed the Marias River on June 12. Sacagawea had been sick for several days, and Clark described her situation as "verry Sick So much So that I move her into the back part of our Covered part of the Perogue which is Cool...." During the day, they encountered several rattlesnakes. Clark wrote "one of the men cought one by the head in Catch'g hold of a bush on which his head lay reclined."

The next day, the main party passed modern-day Shonkin Creek. Clark wrote, "passed a Small rapid Stream...which heads in a mountain to the S.E. 12 or 15 miles, which at this time covered with Snow, we call this stream Snow river, as it is the conveyance of the melted snow from that mountain...." They camped about twelve miles above Shonkin Creek. The sick report for the day was not good. Whitehouse wrote he was very sick with a violent headache. Sacagawea was listed as very sick, one man sick and three others had swellings. Sacagawea was treated with a dose of "Salts."

JUNE 13 - 14, 1805

During the more than two years that the Lewis and Clark Expedition was exploring, a number of days come to mind as being remarkable: such as the day when they first saw the Pacific Ocean, another was the day when McNeal stood astride the westernmost rivulet of the Missouri River. June 13 and June 14, 1805, days spent in the Great Falls area, are two days that similarly stand out in the history of the Expedition.

On June 13, Lewis and the four men were in their third day of walking overland in search of the falls of the Missouri. Lewis' words best describe what happened about noon on this day:

"from the extremity of this roling country I overlooked a most beatifull and level plain of great extent of at least 50 or sixty miles; in this there were infinitely more buffaloe than I had ever before witnessed at a view. nearly in the direction I had been travling or S.W. two curious mountains presented themselves of square figures, the sides rising perpendicularly to the hight of 250 feet [two flat-topped buttes south of Black Horse Lake]....fearing that the river boar to the South and that I might pass the falls if they existed between this an the snowey mountains I altered my course nealy to the South....I had proceded on this course about two miles...whin my ears were saluted with the agreeable sound of a fall of water and advancing a little further I saw the spray arrise above the plain like a collumn of smoke...and heard roaring too tremendious to be mistaken for any cause short of the great falls of the Missouri."

If there had been any earlier doubt about the decision, it was drowned out by a "roaring too tremendious." Although Cruzatte had convinced most of the men that the north fork was the true Missouri, the Captains were not swayed. They had done their homework. The most important piece of evidence the Captains considered was that the Indians had told them they had to go south and west to get to the mountains where the Shoshoni lived on the headwaters and where water drained from one side to the Pacific and from the other to the Missouri. The only doubt in Lewis' mind when he left the Marias was if the south fork originated in mountains other than those separating the two great rivers, otherwise there was no doubt in the Captain's mind. Now with a "roaring too tremendious," all traces of doubt were swept away with the rolling, boiling water as it landed for a brief moment below the rock barrier of the great fall and then passed swiftly from sight.

Lewis hurried down the steep descent of two hundred feet to the base of the great falls where he drank in the scene before him. He called it a "sublimely grand specticle." Lewis' description follows:

"immediately at the cascade the river is about 300 yds. wide; about ninty or a hundred yards of this next the Lard. bluff is a smoth even sheet of water falling over a precipice of at least eighty feet, the remaining part of about 200 yards on my right formes the grandest sight I ever beheld, the hight of the fall is the same of the other but the irregular and somewhat projecting rocks below receives the water in it's passage down and brakes it into a perfect white foam which assumes a thousand forms in a moment sometimes flying up in jets of sparkling foam to the hight of fifteen or twenty feet and are scarcely formed before large roling bodies of the same beaten and foaming water is thrown over and conceals them. in short the rocks seem to be most happily fixed to present a sheet of the whitest beaten froath for 200 yards in length and about 80 feet perpendicular. the water after decending strikes against the

butment before mentioned or that on which I stand and seems to rever-
berate and being met by the more impetuous courant they role and
swell into half formed billows of great hight which rise and again disap-
pear in an instant."

Yet after these wonderful words and many more, Lewis was dis-
satisfied with his inability to see beyond the limits of common-
place experience in conveying his thoughts onto paper and wrote
"after wrighting this imperfect discription I again viewed the
falls and was so much disgusted with the imperfect idea which
it conveyed of the scene that I determined to draw my pen across
it and begin agin...I wished for the pencil of Salvator Rosa or
the pen of Thompson, that I might be enabled to give to the
enlightened world some just idea of this truly magnifficent and
sublimely grand object...."

And the longer he sat there with the mist from the falls wetting
his face, the thought of how inadequate his skills were to prepare a drawing or a written description which would somehow
tell the world back home about this scene crept back into his
journal again. "....I hope still to give to the world some faint
idea of an object which at this moment fills me with such pleasure and astonishment..." When he finally turned his back on
the falls, he held a glimmer of hope that someday with the aid
of his outline of the strong features and his memory that some
artisan could produce a drawing of this wonderful product of
nature. (During Lewis' trip to Philadelphia in 1807, he apparently had a drawing prepared of the falls. A copy of it appeared
in the 1817 Dublin reprint of Biddle and is entitled "Principal
Cascade of the Missouri.")

Sometime during the afternoon, Lewis moved to a wooded area
below the falls where he fixed camp. He felt a certain satisfaction. His efforts at the Marias had led to the right decision and

he wrote that in the morning he would send a man down river to inform Clark and the party of his success in finding the falls and "settle in their minds all further doubts as to the Missouri."

The hunters joined Lewis, bringing in a portion of the meat from three buffalo cows which had been shot about three-quarters of a mile from the falls. The men refreshed themselves for a couple of hours and then three of them went back to bring in another load of meat. Goodrich was directed to cut the meat into thin strips for drying and, after he finished this task, he dropped a fishing line in the river. It was about 4 p.m. when Lewis with his thoughts on how they would portage the falls walked down river for three miles looking for a spot where the canoes could be removed from the water in preparation for their overland trip. Once back at the camp, Lewis described the river as one continual scene of rapids and cascades with the banks steep and rocky sometimes reaching two hundred feet in height. He felt concern about the rugged terrain along the river and how they would get the canoes up the steep banks to the plain.

Goodrich caught a half dozen "very fine trout." From Lewis' description which included the words "a small dash of red on each side behind the front ventral fins," these fish are easily identified as the cutthroat trout. That evening, trout parched in meal, pepper and salt, buffalo humps, tongues and marrowbones were part of the dinner menu which Lewis wrote was "really sumptuous."

June 14, 1805, Lewis was up with the sun. He dispatched Joseph Field with a letter for Captain Clark, ordered one man to build a scaffold for drying meat, sent the others to retrieve more meat from the previous day's kill and, by the close of the day, he would walk close to twenty-four miles, discover four more falls on the river, overlook a "most beatifull and extensive plain" which he called a "ravishing prospect," visit the Sun River and have a foot race with a grizzly bear.

With things organized, Lewis left the camp about 10 a.m. He took his gun and espontoon and planned to walk up river to see where the rapids terminated. About five miles above the great falls, Lewis arrived at a cascade which resulted from a rock shelf nineteen feet high crossing the river in the shape of a horseshoe. Lewis called it Crooked Falls, the name it retains today. Just above this point, the river makes a sharp bend to the north. It was at this point Lewis thought about returning to camp. But his ears picked up a roar inviting him to see what the Missouri had in store up river. He did not have to go far, just a few hundred yards. There the river cascaded over a rock shelf fifty feet high. Lewis wrote it was "one of the most beatifull objects in nature..." And once again, Lewis was challenged to write a description transposing what his eyes saw to what others would see when they read his words. Like at the great falls, several hundred words, wonderfully strung together like no other writer has ever written, found their way onto Lewis' paper.

At this point, Lewis knew he could not turn back even if it meant staying out all night by himself. He was rewarded for continuing his walk. Just a short half mile above the cascade which he called "beautiful cascade" (Rainbow Falls), there was another falls, one that stretched diagonally across the river with a drop of six feet. Lewis wrote "in any other neighbourhood but this, such a cascade would probably be extoled for it's beaty and magnifficence, but here I passed it by with but little attention..."

The river above this small cascade, which in later years would acquire the name of Colter Falls after John Colter of the Expedition, continued to present more rapids and smaller pitches as it turned back to the west. At about two and one half miles from Colter Falls, Lewis found the final falls of the five which collectively make up the great falls of the Missouri River. It was a pitch of twenty-six feet and turned out to be the one the Indians had made special mention of during the previous winter. There below the falls on an island in the middle of the river was the nest of the black eagle which the Indians had described. Lewis felt Black Eagle Falls was "certainly much the greatest" except for those two which he had just described. There was one additional pitch of five feet and after that the river slowed and presented a calm smooth surface.

Lewis climbed the knoll immediately north of Black Eagle Falls and had a view of the expansive inviting plain bordering the river to the west. A short ways from there he could see the river turned to the south. There was no more rock shelving in the river's way to task Lewis' pen for a description. The mountains to the south and southwest were covered with snow. Lewis could see where another river joined the Missouri. He surmised it to be the one the Indians called Medicine River. Vast flocks of geese were feeding on either side of the river. A herd of at least one thousand buffalo was grazing near the southern bend in the river. It was a "ravishing prospect," unlike anything the Virginia native would have ever seen in his home state. He feasted his eyes on the scene for a few minutes as he rested.

Having come this far, Lewis wanted to continue on to see the river called Medicine River (Sun River). As he passed the bend in the Missouri, he decided to kill a buffalo to provide dinner if he had to spend the night away from camp. As he watched the buffalo fall to the ground, "a large white, or reather brown bear...crept on me within 20 steps...." At the moment he saw the bear, Lewis also remembered he had failed to reload his rifle.

The bear running "open mouthed and full speed" chased Lewis for eighty yards. With the bear beginning to take charge of the race, Lewis decided on a different course of action. He ran into the water up to his waist and turned with his espontoon in hand to meet the bear in combat. The bear came to the edge of the water, twenty feet from Lewis and "sudonly wheeled about as if frightened...and retreated with quite as great precipitation as he had just before pursued me."

Lewis got back to the shore and immediately reloaded his gun. He silently vowed to himself to never allow his firearm to be empty of a charge. Once the bear declined combat, it ran at full speed toward the Sun River, on occasion looking back to see if the strange creature was pursuing. Lewis was not deterred and followed the bear towards the Sun, which Lewis called a "handsome stream, about 200 yds wide with a gentle current, apparently deep, it's water clear..."

On the way back to camp, Lewis came upon an animal he described as a burrowing tiger cat (perhaps a wolverine or badger). He took a shot at it, but the animal retreated to its hole. In continuing his route, Lewis then had three bull buffalo charge him. Lewis altered his course to the direction of the charging bulls. He thought "at least to give them some amusement..." His tactic worked. The bulls rushed to about a hundred yards from the Captain where they, like the grizzly bear, then retreated in a hurry.

As he walked in the fading twilight, he thought the day might have all been a dream, but the thorns of the prickly pear cactus penetrating his moccasins reminded him it was real. It was well past dark when Lewis finally got back to camp. The men were very worried about their leader and had already planned routes each would take in the morning to search for him. Lewis wrote that evening, "It now seemed to me that all the beasts of the neighbourhood had made a league to distroy me, or that some fortune was disposed to amuse herself at my expence..." June 14, 1805 was a warm day. Lewis had left his leather overshirt at the falls and had worn only his yellow flannel shirt.

Late in the afternoon of June 14, Joseph Field arrived where Clark's party was on the river and gave Lewis' letter to Clark. The red-haired Captain read the letter dated from the great falls of the Missouri; it informed the Expedition members the falls Lewis had found answered the description given by the Indians. The eagle's nest was there. The Captains had made the right decision.

The good news did not make life easier for Clark and his party. He wrote they made only ten miles that day because "the Current excesevely rapid more So as we assend we find great difficuelty in getting the Perogue & Canoes up in Safety, Canoes take in water frequently." The Indian woman had complained all night and was near death. Two men had toothaches, two men had tumors and one man had a tumor and a fever.

JUNE 15 - 16, 1805

The going did not improve for Clark and his crew. The next day, June 15, he wrote: "we can hear the falls this morning verry distinctly.... the curt. excessively rapid and dificuelt to assend great numbers of dangerous places, and the fatigue which we have to encounter is incretiatable the men in the water from morning untill night hauling the Cord & boats walking on Sharp rocks and round Sliperery Stones which alternately cut their feet & throw them down..."

Besides the difficult traveling conditions, the Indian woman was "much wors this evening, She will not take any medison." And in the midst of all this, her husband Charbonneau, petitioned to return home. During the 15th, they passed a small river entering the Missouri from the mountains to the southeast. Clark called it Shield's River after John Shields; Gass, Ordway and Whitehouse called it Strawberry Creek. Today it is known as Highwood Creek. After the party halted for the day, Clark sent Joseph Field back to Lewis' camp near the great falls to inform his fellow captain of his location.

June 15, Lewis took some time off to recurperate from the harried pace he set for the past four days. He kept the men busy hauling meat to camp to be dried. He fished some with Goodrich, but mostly he slept. When he awoke from his day sleep he found a prairie rattlesnake coiled near the trunk of the tree under which he had been laying. The snake was about ten feet away and was soon dispatched by Lewis. Joseph Field arrived late that evening and relayed the location of Clark. Lewis then directed the young man to be prepared to return to Clark's camp in the morning. He was to tell Clark to send men for the meat dried by Lewis' party.

Finally, on the 16th, Clark reached a point where the river turned into a series of cascades reaching as far as he could see. The party halted at this point, and Clark "walked up on the Lard Side as high as a large Creek, which falls in on the Lard. Side one mile above & opposit a large Sulpher Spring...." Sacagawea was closer than ever to death.

On June 16, Joseph Field left early for Clark's camp with the message to send back a party of men for the meat. It was Field's third trip as messenger between the two Captains. The party arrived about noon at Lewis' camp, picked up the six hundred pounds of dried meat and with Lewis returned to Clark's camp on the west side of the river, arriving about 2 p.m. After Lewis arrived from the falls, Lower Portage Camp was established on the east side of the river, three quarters of a mile south of Clark's camp of June 15. Lewis stayed on the west side the night of June 16 to direct the transfer of the canoes up river.

PLANS FOR THE PORTAGE

The two Captains now rejoined at Clark's camp discussed the falls and the portage that would have to be made to continue upstream. There was no hesitation. They reviewed the possibilities. Lewis wrote: "I now informed Capt. C. of my discoveries with rispect to the most proper side for our portage, and of it's great length, which I could not estimate at less than 16 miles. Capt. C. had already sent two men this morning to examine the country on the S. side of the river."

The report of the two men sent by Clark to explore the south side of the river was "very unfavourable. they informed us that the creek just above us and two deep ravenes still higher up cut the plain between the river and the mountain in such a manner, that in their opinions a portage for the canoes on this side was impracticable." The Captains answer to their report was simple: "g[o]od or bad we must make the portage." It was not a matter of choice.

It most likely never occurred to Lewis it would be just one day short of a month before he would be back in the water in search of the headwaters of the Missouri. From their conversations with the Indians of the Mandan area, Lewis and Clark had expected to make a half-day portage around the falls. They now realized this would not be possible. Arrangements had to be made to get the heavy canoes and their baggage around the falls, and from his exploration on June 14, Lewis knew the best choice for the portage was the south side of the Missouri. With the big bend in the river, it would be shorter and, other than the two deep ravines, it was mostly rolling country. Lewis wrote, "as the distance was too great to think of transporting the canoes and baggage on the men's shoulders, we scelected six men...to set about making a parsel of truck wheels in order to convey our canoes and baggage over the portage." The Captains' pirogue could not be portaged. It would have to be left below the falls and the iron frame canoe would be assembled to take its place.

The Captains decided to make their camp about one mile below the entrance of Belt Creek on the east side of the river. There was "sufficient quantity of wood [driftwood] for fuel, an article which can be obtained but in few places in this neighbourhood." Lewis had had an excellent view of this stretch of the river when he walked down from the falls. Perhaps it was during this walk that he decided how they would get the canoes out of the river, up the steep banks to the level plain where the men could get them on the make-shift carts to be dragged overland to where they could get back into the waters of the Missouri.

The pieces of the portage puzzle fell into place. Lewis had seen Belt Creek on his walk from the falls. Clark had explored it upon his arrival in the area. Singularly or together, it was decided the canoes could be moved up Belt Creek to avoid the steep banks of the Missouri. The canoes which were on the west side of the river had to be taken to the east bank and the baggage unloaded at the Lower Portage Camp. So on June 16, the canoes were passed over to the east side of the river, unloaded and then passed back over to the west side. The night of June 16, Clark was camped at Lower Portage Camp, while Lewis was camped across the river to direct the movement of the canoes up the west bank to Belt Creek. The men then pulled the canoes along the west bank until they had them above the rapid at the mouth of Belt Creek. Just above this rapid, the canoes were passed to the east bank and then into Belt Creek. They could then be pulled up Belt Creek where it was hoped a gentle slope leading to the plain above the Missouri River could be found. Belt Creek was the passageway through the steep river bluffs on which the canoes could be moved to the plain above the river.

The Expedition arrived at Belt Creek with six canoes and the Captains' white pirogue. The decision to leave the white pirogue here was made perhaps as early as the previous winter at Fort Mandan. After all, Lewis had been gathering hides for his iron frame canoe since before the Expedition arrived at the mouth of the Marias River. (Lewis actually had started collecting hides the previous winter in Mandan, but these hides spoiled and had to be discarded.) And once they arrived in the area, they saw there was no practical way to get the pirogue up Belt Creek, and it was just as impractical to think they could haul it eighteen or so miles overland. Lewis wrote on June 18: "This morning I employed all hands in drawing the perogue on shore in a thick bunch of willow bushes some little distance below our camp; fastened her securely, drove out the plugs of the gage holes of her bottom and covered her with bushes and driftwood to shelter her from the sun."

LEWIS AND CLARK'S PORTAGE CREEK

Entering the Missouri River below Morony Dam, Belt Creek drains the Little Belt Mountains, southeast of Great Falls. Lewis called it Portage Creek because it served as the first leg of the Expedition's portage around the falls. Near the community of Belt, there is a dome-shaped hill with a girdle or belt of rock outcropping and from this, the creek and nearby mountains got their names. When the Expedition first arrived in the area of Belt Creek, it was called "Red Creek" because of the red cliffs which line the drainage. In the eyes of the 1805 explorers, the name "Portage Creek" was apparently preferable to "Red Creek."

Expedition members dragged the canoes one and three-quarters miles up Belt Creek to a level spot where they were allowed to dry in the sun. Whitehouse indicated the canoes were removed from Belt Creek just as soon as the steep cliffs gave way and moved on carriages to the spot where they were left to dry in the sun. From this point, the canoes were put on the wagons and taken up a gradual ascent to a staging area on the plain. The men then pulled and pushed the wagons to White Bear Islands where the Expedition was again able to take to the water.

Without the Belt Creek access, the task of getting the canoes from the Missouri River bottom to the plain above would have been impractical in this area. As it was, the men experienced much difficulty in getting them over the rocks and rapids of Belt Creek during spring runoff. One of the canoes overturned and a man was nearly drowned. Lewis wrote that "just above the canoes (where they were overturned to dry) the creek has a perpendicular fall of 5 feet and the cliffts again become very steep and high." Whitehouse described the effort it took to get the canoes up Belt Creek: "In the Evening we got our Crafts up the small River to the falls of it, which was about 8 feet perpendicular, and the Water running very rapid down them,—We experienc'd much difficulty, as well as danger in getting our Crafts up the rapids this day.— One of our craft turned upside down

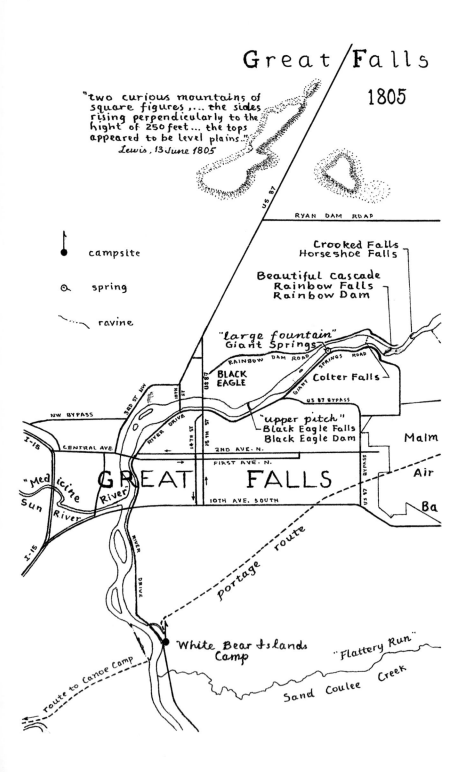

Great Falls
1805

"two curious mountains of square figures,... the sides rising perpendicularly to the hight of 250 feet... the tops appeared to be level plains.."
Lewis, 13 June 1805

RYAN DAM ROAD

● campsite

⊙ spring

⌁ ravine

Crooked Falls
Horseshoe Falls

Beautiful Cascade
Rainbow Falls
Rainbow Dam

"large fountain"
Giant Springs

RAINBOW DAM ROAD

BLACK EAGLE

GIANT SPRINGS ROAD

Colter Falls

US 87 BYPASS

"upper pitch"
Black Eagle Falls
Black Eagle Dam

NW BYPASS

32ND ST NW

19TH ST

US 87

RIVER DRIVE

14TH ST

15TH ST

2ND AVE. N.

FIRST AVE. N.

Malm

Air

Ba

I-15

CENTRAL AVE.

"Medicine

Sun River

Sun River

GREAT FALLS

10TH AVE. SOUTH

US 87 BYPASS

I-15

RIVER DRIVE

portage route

route to Canoe Camp

White Bear Islands Camp

"Flattery Run"

Sand Coulee Creek

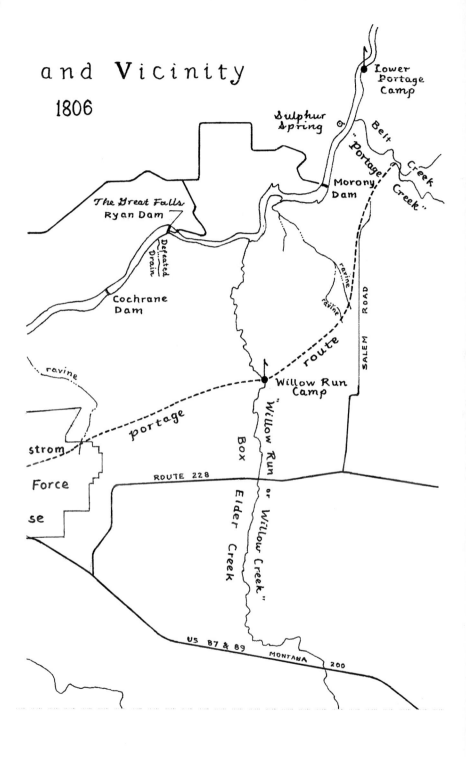

& the 2 Men that were in her narrowly escaped being drownded, several others of them filled with water. With much difficulty & fataigue we hawled those Crafts on our carriages up to where the falls commenced, and took them up the bank, out to a level piece of Ground, and turned them up on their edges to dry, We encamped here for this night, all our party being much fataigued." The day was June 17.

Sergeant Patrick Gass and five others felled the only tree of any size in the area and from it cut wheels for the two carriages. Lewis wrote, "we were fortunate enough to find one cotton-wood tree just below the entrance of portage creek that was large enough to make carrage wheels about 22 Inches in diameter; fortunate I say because I do not beleive that we could find another of the same size perfectly sound within 20 miles of us." The mast of the white pirogue was made into two axeltrees and cottonwood although soft and brittle was used for the other parts of the carriages. Once the portage was over, the wheels were cached at White Bear Islands and used again during the 1806 portage.

From June 16 to June 28, the Expedition maintained a camp about one mile below Belt Creek. This camp was referred to as the Lower Portage Camp and from it, Captain Clark organized and directed the eleven-day portage. A smaller canoe which was used to cross the river to Sulphur Springs and to hunt on the north side of the river was kept in this area until the final portage trip. Lewis set up camp near White Bear Islands and remained there during most of the time the Expedition was in the Great Falls area.

CLARK'S SURVEY OF THE PORTAGE ROUTE

Besides the two major questions: How to get the canoes from the river to the plains? and Which side of the river offered the best portage opportunity? The other question was: What is the best route to White Bear Islands? The Captains could have had the men simply start across the plain in the general direction of where the river turns back to the south. But this is not what happened. The portage route was determined before the men started overland. On June 16, Clark wrote, "I deturmined to examine & Survey the Portage find a leavel rout if possible—"

Clark left at 8 o'clock on the morning of June 17. He and the five men (Willard, Colter, others unidentified) who were assigned to accompany him took four days to explore the south side of the river and identify the best location for the portage route. His course took him up Belt Creek "Some distance to examine that & if possable assend that Sufficently high, that a Streight cours to the mouth of Medison river would head the 2 reveins...." In examining Belt Creek, he found only one gentle slope leading from the drainage to the plains above. Above this point, the banks are steep and rocky. It was not possible to move the canoes further up Belt Creek to a point perpendicular to the head of the two ravines. Once this part of the route was resolved, Clark and the five men crossed the plain in a southwest direction in an attempt to find the head of the two deep cuts the two men had told the Captains about on the previous day. Once they found the start of the two ravines, Clark then turned north intending to reach the river at the "great pitch." His path brought him to the Missouri River where the second drainage Willow Creek or Run enters the river. No words but his own can best describe Clark's walk up the Missouri towards the great falls.

"we proceeded up the river passing a Sucession of rapids&Cascades to the Falls, which we had herd for Several miles makeing a dedly Sound, I beheld those Cateracts with astonishment the whole of the water of this great river Confined in a Channel of 280 yards and pitching over a rock of 97 feet 3/4 of an, from the foot of the falls arrises a Continued mist which is extended for 150 yds down & to near the top of the Clifts on LSd. the river below is Confined a narrow Chanl. of 93 yards haveing a Small bottom of timber on the Stard Side which is defined by a rock, rangeing Cross wise the river a little below the Shoot, a Short distance below this Cataract a large rock divides the Stream, I in assendending the Clifts to take the hith of the fall was near Slipping into the water, at which place I must have been Sucked under in an instant, and with deficuelty and great risque I assended again, and decended the Clift lower down (but few places Can be descended to the river) and took the hight with as much accuricy as possible with a Spirit Leavels &c."

After climbing about on the steep rocky river bank, Clark and his men found a spring two hundred yards below the great falls where "4 Cotton willow trees grew." Here they dined and Clark as he did several times during the Expedition carved his name (and height of the falls) on one of the trees.

The party worked its way back to the plain and proceeded up the river to a deep draw just below Crooked Falls where they camped for the night. Clark noted in his journal the night was cold and the mountains in every direction had snow on them.

The next morning, Clark arrived early at the second great cataract. Here he had no trouble reaching the river bottom below the falls where he measured the drop at 47 feet, 8 inches with the width of the river at 473 yards. In describing this falls (Rainbow), Clark borrowed words from Lewis when he wrote that it is "one of the grandest views in nature and by far exceeds any thing I ever Saw..." He measured the smaller falls above Rainbow Falls at 14 feet 7 inches. From here, he and the five men followed the river for a little over a mile where they came upon a large spring about eight feet from the river's edge. Clark wrote this was the largest spring he had ever seen and speculated it might be the largest in America. Clark called it the "Large Fountain." Today it is known as Giant Springs, a name given to it by Paris Gibson, the founder of the city of Great Falls, and the area around it is a beautiful state park. The spring discharges more than 170 million gallons of water every 24 hours.

A short distance above the spring, Clark measured Black Eagle Falls at 26 feet 5 inches with the river being 580 yards wide. He wrote "this fall is not intirely perpdincular a Short bench gives a Curve to the water as it falls." The party killed a buffalo cow and took as much meat as needed to a grove of trees opposite where the Sun River enters the Missouri. Clark wrote at this point the Missouri was 800 yards wide. (Bergantino feels this should be 300 yards. This is either a mistake on Clark's part or on that of the editors. Clark's maps in Moulton Volume 4 and Volume 1 show the distance as 300. Clark's triangulation yields about 300 yards. Perhaps a "3" was read as an "8.")

Clark and his party spent the rest of June 18 and all day June 19 exploring the country and the river to the south. About four miles above the point where the Sun River enters the Missouri, Clark found a small creek he called "Flattery Run," (Sand Coulee Creek). On his walk to Sand Coulee Creek, he passed three islands. These islands were home to a population of grizzly bears that were called "white bears" due to their frost-colored pelage. Over the course of the next month, these white bears provided various members of the Expedition with headline stories to share with the folks back home. Clark's imagination did not have to struggle when it searched for a name for these islands which he had determined to be the ending point of the portage. He wrote after exploring the area on the 19th, "I returned to Camp late and deturmined that the best nearest and most eassy rout would be from the lower part of the 3rd or white bear Island...." Before he closed out his journal for the day, he wrote about something which anyone who has been in the Great Falls area for a brief time knows about, "the wind all this day blew violently hard....I lost a part of my notes which could not be found as the wind must have blown them to a great distance."

Clark had stakes cut to be stuck in the ground as guideposts for the men as they moved across the plains with the canoes and baggage. During the morning of June 19, Clark and the five men staked the route to the point where they met the first deep ravine (Willow Run). Here Clark was concerned about how they would get the carriages up and down its steep banks. He spent time looking for a way around it. Finally as the day was getting late, he turned north walked to the river and eventually arrived back at Lower Portage Camp. Included in his journal for the day was that the idea of sending one canoe and some of the men back to St. Louis from the falls had been abandoned by the Captains. It was now obvious all thirty-one men were needed. As Clark wrote: "we have never hinted to any one of the party that we had Such a Scheem in contemplation, and all appear perfectly to have made up their minds, to Succeed in the expedition or perish in the attempt. we all believe that we are about to enter on the most perilous and dificuelt part of our Voyage, yet I See no one repineing; all appear ready to meet those dificuelties which await us with resolution and becomeing fortitude."

THE NOISE

During their stay in this area, members of the Expedition repeatedly heard a loud rumbling sound originating in the mountains drained by the Sun River. Lewis described it as "resembling precisely the discharge of a piece of ordinance of 6 pounds at the distance of three miles."

Initially the captains were not impressed with the noise, and believed it to be thunder. Others of the party, however, were convinced that it was not thunder. Clark said, "I was informed of it Several times by the men J. Fields particularly before I paid any attention to it, thinking it was thunder most probably which they had mistaken."

Once the captains began to listen for it, they remembered the Indians of Fort Mandan had talked about "a great noise" made by the Rocky Mountains. The river which drained the mountains from where the noise originated was called the Medicine River by the Indians because they could not explain the origin of the sound.

As noted by Lewis and Clark, they had no explanation for this phenomenon. It was heard at different times both at night and during the day. Sometimes, it was a single sound, while at other times it was, as Clark described: "Several discharges in quick Succession."

Lewis wrote the area contained a list of "prodegies...which nature seems to have dealt with a liberal hand, for I have scarcely experienced a day since my first arrival in this quarter without experiencing some novel occurrence among the party or witnessing the appearance of some uncommon object." He wrote these words on his way to visit the Giant Fountain and surely on this list he would have included the "noise."

SACAGAWEA

Of all the members of the Lewis and Clark Expedition, Sacagawea has had more memorials and more statues built in her honor than anyone else. Mountains in three states are named for her. A gold-colored dollar coin carries an image of her. Outside of the Captains, she is the most recognized member of the 1804-1806 Expedition.

She was probably not more than seventeen years old when she traveled with Lewis and Clark. The only firsthand information we have of her is what is recorded in the Expedition's journals.

Sacagawea was a member of the Shoshoni or Snake Indian Tribe of Idaho and western Montana. As a young girl, she had been captured by the Minnetaree or Hidatsa Indians and taken to the Fort Mandan area. Here she was married to Toussaint Charbonneau, a French-Canadian. On February 11, 1805, two months before leaving with the Expedition, Sacagawea gave birth to a boy, Jean Baptiste. Lewis wrote that the first-time mother was experiencing difficulty in delivering the baby, so on the advice of René Jessaume (a trader living with the Mandan Indians), he offered her a powder which was made by crushing the rattle from a rattlesnake. Lewis just happened to have a rattle in his pocket, so he was able to follow the advice of Jessaume. Within minutes, the baby was born. There is no evidence supporting this medicinal remedy. Lewis also had his doubts. "Whether this medicine was truly the cause or not I shall not undertake to determine, but I was informed that she had not taken it more than ten minutes before she brought forth perhaps this remedy may be worthy of future experiments, but I must confess that I want faith as to its efficacy."

During the winter at Fort Mandan, Lewis and Clark learned they would need horses to cross the mountains and the Shoshoni Indians who lived near the mountains had horses. They hired Charbonneau as an interpreter with his wife, Sacagawea, listed in the journals as "interpretress." When they decided to include Sacagawea, the Captains certainly were aware of the possible benefit she could be to them in dealing with the Shoshoni. During the time Sacagawea was ill in the Great Falls area, Lewis explained her role as "the consideration of her being our only dependence for a friendly negociation with Snake Indians on whom we depend for horses to assist us in our portage from the Missouri to the columbia River." There is little doubt Lewis saw the young Indian as one of the pieces to complete the puzzle.

The Corps of Discovery was not long from Fort Mandan when the journalists noted Sacagawea "busied herself in serching for the wild artichokes *(Helian tuberosus)* which the mice collect and deposit in large hoards." Employing the Indian method of poking the earth with a sharp stick in and around drift wood to find the stashes of the mice, the young woman found the roots which, as Lewis wrote, tasted like Jerusalem articokes. In early May as the Expediton reached the Milk River, Sacagawea collected wild liquorice *(Glycyrrhiza lepidota)* and the white apple *(Psoralea esculenta)*. The white apple would became a staple of the men's diet while the Expedition worked its way across the plains of eastern and central Montana.

On May14, Sacagawea was center stage during an incident which is fondly repeated by modern students as having saved the journals of the Expedition. Her husband was at the helm of the Captain's pirogue when a gust of wind hit the sail and turned the pirogue sideways threatening to over turn her. Panic struck Charbonneau. And it was only when Cruzatte took charge and threatened to shoot the Frenchman if he did not take hold of the rudder and do as he was told did the pirogue come under control. Two days later, Lewis recorded in his journal that the articles which had gotten wet were dried and that only some of the medicine items were destroyed by becoming wet. He wrote: "the ballance of our losses consisted of some gardin seeds, a small quantity of gunpowder, and a few culinary articles which fell overboard and sunk, the Indian woman to whom I ascribe equal fortitude and resolution, with any person onboard at the time of the accedent, caught and preserved most of the light articles which were washed overboard." We know the journals were among the items kept on the white pirogue, but we do not know if the pieces of paper on which the Captains and others wrote were among those items washed overboard. The journalists including Lewis do not mention the journals as being among the items saved by the Indian woman.

On May 20, a river was named for her and Lewis recorded her name—Sâh-câ-gar me-âh. With this first attempt to arrange English letters to reflect the way she pronounced her name, the discussion about how to spell and pronounce it is yet to conclude. This river in Petroleum County was for many years called Crooked Creek; it has now been named Sacajawea River.

When they met the Shoshoni Indians in the Lemhi Pass area, one of the most remarkable quirks of fate happened. Lewis had gone ahead of the main party in search of the Shoshoni Indians and had found them in the country near present-day Salmon,

Idaho. When Clark and the main party arrived, Lewis described what happened. "Shortly after Capt. Clark arrived with the Interpreter Charbono, and the Indian woman, who proved to be a sister of the Chif Cameahwait. the meeting of those people was really affecting, particularly between Sah cah-gar-we-ah and an Indian woman, who had been taken prisoner at the same time with her, and who had afterwards escaped from the Minnetares and rejoined her nation."

Nicholas Biddle in the first official publication of the Lewis and Clark journals (1814) described the reunion in much detail: "We soon drew near to the camp, and just as we approached it a woman made her way through the crowd towards Sacajawea, and recognising each other, they embraced with the most tender affection. The meeting of these two young women had in it something peculiarly touching, not only in the ardent manner in which their feelings were expressed, but from the real interest of their situation. They had been companions in childhood, in the war with the Minnetarees they had both been taken prisoners in the same battle, they had shared and softened the rigours of their captivity, till one of them had escaped from the Minnetarrees, with scarce a hope of ever seeing her friend relieved from the hands of her enemies." Clark and Lewis were invited to take part in a ceremony under a covering made of willows. Once the smoking was completed, Sacagawea was brought into the shade to assist with interpreting. Biddle wrote "she came into the tent, sat down, and was beginning to interpret, when in the person of Cameahwait she recognised her brother: she instantly jumped up, and ran and embraced him, throwing over him her blanket and weeping profusely: the chief was himself moved, though not in the same degree. After some conversation between them she resumed her seat, and attempted to interpret for us, but her new situation seemed to overpower her, and she was frequently interrupted by her tears."

Writers after the Expedition created the legend that Sacagawea served as a guide for Lewis and Clark. Eva Emery Dye was in search of a woman to serve as the heroine for the woman's suffrage movement of the early 1900's. Dye settled on Sacagawea and her book *Conquest the True Story of Lewis and Clark* launched the young woman into stardom. Later, Grace Raymond Hebard in the book *Sacagawea, Guide of the Lewis and Clark Expedition* added to the story. The legend grew with the support of a number of statues and paintings showing her pointing the way.

On only two occasions did Sacagawea provide direct geographic assistance. In 1806, after Clark's party had traveled through the Gibbon Pass area, she confirmed Clark's decision to follow the Indian route through the Big Hole Pass, a shorter and easier way to where the canoes had been left in 1805. In the Gallatin Valley, Clark at first considered going through Bridger Pass, but Sacagawea pointed out the southern (Bozeman) pass to the Yellowstone River. Clark wrote, "The indian woman who has been of great Service to me as a pilot through this country recommends a gap in the mountain more south which I shall cross."

Sacagawea's presence signaled to the many Indians whom they met that the Expedition was not a war party, a circumstance beneficial to Lewis and Clark in their encounters with the Indians, and on several occasions, she fulfilled her official role as "interpretress." In dealing with the Shoshoni, Lewis wrote, "through the medium of Labuish, Charbono and Sah-cah-gar-weah, we communicated to them fully...." The Captains also asked her about things she saw, plants, animals, Indian items found by members of the Expedition, so in this role, she served as a "consultant."

Sacagawea's fate after the Expedition has been subject to much discussion. Most modern day students rely on John Luttig, a merchant clerk at Fort Manuel near Pierre, South Dakota who wrote in his journal on December 20, 1812, "this evening the Wife of Charbonneau, a Snake Squaw, died of a putrid fever she was a good and the best woman in the fort, aged abt 25 years she left a fine infant girl." Clark made an inventory of Expedition members in the 1820's and he recorded Sacagawea as being among those Expedition members who were dead.

WHITE PUDDINGS and PRAIRIE APPLES

The bulb of the prairie plant *Psoralea esculenta,* commonly called prairie apple, white apple or breadroot, was described by Lewis as "tastless insipid food of itself tho' I have no doubt but it is a very healthy and moderately nutricious food." The bulbs were used extensively by the plains Indians. They were collected in late summer, strung on cords and allowed to dry in the sun. They could then be used to thicken soup. The bulbs were also eaten in the green state or boiled with meat.

When Sacagawea recovered from her illness, she gathered the white apples in the vicinity of Lower Portage Camp and ate a number of these bulbs without any preparation. She became ill again and complained of her condition, much to the dismay of Lewis, who had just gotten her back on her feet. He wrote, "she walked out and gathered a considerable quantity of the white apples of which she eat so heartily in their raw state, together with a considerable quantity of dryed fish without my knowledge that she complained very much and her fever again returned. I rebuked Sharbono serverely for suffering her to indulge herself with such food he being privey to it and having been previously told what she must only eat."

Although Lewis was not fond of eating prairie apples, he was quite taken with a dish prepared by Sacagawea's husband. Charbonneau's primary role was to interpret for Lewis and Clark, but once the Expedition was underway, his cooking skills earned him another duty. Lewis wrote: "from the cow I killed we saved the necessary materials for making what our wrighthand cook Charbono calls the boudin blanc, and immediately set him about preparing them for supper; this white pudding we all esteem one of the greatest delacies...." This esteemed delicacy consisted of stuffing meat, kidney suet, flour, salt and pepper into a scantily washed six-foot section of the "lowere extremity of the large gut of the Buffaloe...." After a brief dip in the Missouri, the stuffed gut was boiled and then fried in bear's grease until brown. It was then "ready to esswage the pangs of a keen appetite" as Lewis described it.

THE 1805 PORTAGE

The Indians of the Fort Mandan country had told Lewis and Clark about the falls of the Missouri River and that a portage around them would require about a half day. As Lewis discovered on June 14, 1805, there were five falls. A month's time was consumed as the Expedition portaged the canoes and equipment and got ready to continue up the Missouri to the Rocky Mountains.

The portage route established by Clark on the south side of the river covered about eighteen miles from Lower Portage Camp to White Bear Islands. The route crossed the plains through what is now farmland, Malmstrom Air Force Base, the southwest part of the City of Great Falls and the corner of Mount Olivet Cemetery. While Clark was surveying the route, Lewis remained at Lower Portage Camp assigning duties to the men in anticipation of Clark's return and the start of the portage.

On June 18 after the white pirogue was taken out of service, Lewis had all of the Expedition's goods lain out on the ground so they could be inspected and re-packed for the portage. Items destined for the cache were set aside. He paid particular attention to the frame of his iron canoe and found one screw was missing and it had suffered some rust. John Shields, the Expedition's blacksmith, fabricated a screw.

Lewis directed Drouillard, Reubin Field and Shannon to the north side of the river to hunt in the area of the Sun River. It was Lewis' intent to build up a supply of dried meat at Lower Portage Camp to feed the men during the portage. This would allow as many men as possible to haul the canoes and baggage.

The portage began June 21. Clark had returned the evening before and explained that the route was across the plains a considerable distance from the river and there was only one place where the men would be able to find water. From Willow Run to the White Bear Islands, there was no water. This meant the portage had to be completed in a day. To give the men as much of a chance as possible to accomplish this task, the Captains had what ever was to be portaged the next day taken to a staging area on the plain the day before. Lewis wrote: "This morning I employed the greater part of the men in transporting a part of the bagage over portage creek to the top of the high plain about three miles in advance on the portage. I also had one canoe carryed on truck wheles to the same place and put the baggage in it, in order to make an early start in the morning...." The baggage was carried by the men up the steep bank of the Missouri River immediately south of where Belt Creek enters it. The baggage and canoes were then ready for an early start to White Bear Islands. From this staging spot on the plain above the Missouri, it was about fifteen miles to the ending point of the portage.

Undoubtedly, Lewis worried about the effort required to get all of the goods transported around the falls. But he knew it would get done; however, the worries about assembling the iron frame canoe nagged him like a just-weaned puppy dog. He knew there was a good chance he could not make it work and some other answer would have to be found for the white pirogue's replacement. So with the first load of goods destined for White Bear Islands, Lewis had his personal items, the iron frame of his experimental canoe and the baggage of three men to assemble it included.

On Saturday June 22, the men strapped on the harnesses and began to pull the two carriages across the plain first in a southerly direction and then in a southwesterly direction to White Bear Islands. Ordway, Goodrich, Charbonneau, York and Sacagawea remained at Lower Portage Camp. One carriage carried a canoe, the other was loaded with baggage. By noon, the party had reached the drainage called Willow Run. Here they dined, drank water and repaired axeltrees, tongues and hounds of the carriages. The white pirogue's mast and cottonwood tongues and cross bars had broken several times. It was dark when the party got within a half mile of the White Bear Islands. The tongue broke on the carriage with the canoe, so the men took what baggage they could on their backs and proceeded to the Islands. Lewis wrote "each man took as much of the bagagge as he could carry on his back and proceeded to the river where we formed our encampment much fortiegued." When Clark had explored the area for the end point of the portage, he had had the men kill several animals for meat to be left for the portaging party. The wolves unaware of Clark's intentions helped themselves to the choice cuts and left only scraps for the humans. The men arrived exhausted with just enough energy to curse the wolves and eat the leftovers. Clark wrote, "a number of wolves...had distroyed a great part of our meat which I had left at that place when I was up day before yesterday we Soon went to Sleep & Slept Sound...."

Sometime during the day of June 23, Lewis wrote those often repeated words about just how damn hard it was for the men to move the Expeditions goods from Lower Portage Camp to White Bear Islands:

> "—during the late rains the buffaloe have troden up the praire very much, which having now become dry the sharp points of earth as hard as frozen ground stand up in such abundance that there is no avoiding them. this is particulary severe on the feet of the men who have not only their own wight to bear in treading on those hacklelike points but have also the

addition of the burthen which they draw and which in fact is as much as they can possibly move with. they are obliged to halt and rest frequently for a few minutes, at every halt these poor fellows tumble down and are so much fatiegued that many of them are asleep in an instant; in short their fatiegues are incredible; some are limping from the soreness of their feet, others faint and unable to stand for a few minutes, with heat and fatiegue, yet no one complains, all go with cheerfullness."

The next morning, the canoe and the rest of the baggage were brought to camp. Then Clark had the men start back with the empty carriages. Once back at Belt Creek, he had two canoes taken to the staging area on the plain in preparation for the next day's trip. On the way back to Lower Portage Camp, he made additional measurements and straightened the route from what they had followed on the first trip. He had the men drive stakes in the ground to mark the route. Anxious to get started on his iron frame canoe, Lewis had the three men with him clear a place under some "shady willows" for the project. In the afternoon, he and Joseph Field took the canoe down to the Sun River to check on the hunters.

Lewis and Field walked up the starboard (north) side of the Sun River, "hooping frequently" as they went to attract the attention of the hunters. Five miles up river, they found George Shannon whom Lewis had directed to leave the great falls on June 19 and proceed to the Sun River to hunt elk. The young man who would one day become a state senator in Missouri had killed seven deer, several buffalo, but no elk. He had six hundred pounds of dried meat. It was too late for Lewis to return to White Bear Islands, so they constructed a raft and crossed the Sun River to Shannon's camp for the night.

The morning of June 24, Clark was up early. He had the remaining canoe taken from the water and the remaining baggage divided into three parcels. One parcel of baggage and the canoe were taken up Belt Creek to where the other canoes were drying. Once this was accomplished, Clark and the men started the second trip to White Bear Islands. This time, they took two canoes and the one parcel of baggage. Clark wrote "I accompany them 4 miles and returned, my feet being verry Sore from the walk over ruts Stones & hills & thro the leavel plain for 6 days proceeding Carrying my pack and gun."

The second trip to White Bear Islands went much better than the first one. A storm wet the ground and added to the difficulties of pushing and pulling the carriages, but it was one of those somewhat rare days when the wind blows from the northeast and on June 24, 1805, the Lewis and Clark men took full advantage of it. Clark recorded "it may be here worthy of remark that the Sales were hoised in the Canoes as the men were drawing them and the wind was great relief to them being Sufficently Strong to move the Canoes on the Trucks, this is Saleing on Dry land in every Sence of the word."

Clark was feeling under the weather with a case of "looseness" on June 25. He assigned Charbonneau the only man with him at Lower Portage Camp to have dinner ready for the men who would be returning from White Bear Islands. Clark wrote he had a "little Coffee for brackfast which was to me a riarity as I had not tasted any Since last winter." He went on to give us a sense of what the area was like: "This Countrey has a romantick appearance river inclosed between high and Steep hills Cut to pieces by revines but little timber and that Confined to the Rivers & Creek, the Missourie has but a fiew Scattering trees on its borders, and only one Solitary Cotton tree in sight of my Camp the wood which we burn is drift wood which is broken to pieces in passing the falls, not one large tree longer than about 8 or 10 feet to be found drifted below the falls the plains are inferior in point of Soil to those below, more Stone on the sides of the hill, grass but a few inches high and but few flowers in the Plains, great quantites of Choke Cheries, Goose burres, red & yellow berries, & red & Purple Currents on the edges of water....bluffs are a hard red or redish brown earth Containing Iron. we Catch great quantities of Trout...."

The party from White Bear Islands got back to Lower Portage Camp in time to get one canoe and some baggage to the staging point on the plain. Afterwards, Cruzatte got out his violin and played music to which the men danced about on the dirt floor.

The men started early on June 26 to make their third trip to White Bear Islands. This time they took two canoes and baggage which, according to Ordway, consisted of "pearched meal pork powder lead axes tools Bisquit and portable soup." Clark remained at Lower Portage Camp where he prepared items including Lewis' desk to be left in the cache. The swivel gun (mountain howitzer) was left under some rocks. The two blunderbusses were put in the cache. Charbonneau was assigned to fill empty kegs with buffalo tallow. And both Captains recorded in their journals that Lewis' plant collection from Mandan to the falls was deposited in the cache at Lower Portage Camp. But in 1806, Lewis wrote that it was in the cache at White Bear Islands.

The men returned the next day June 27 to Lower Portage Camp by 4 p.m. After a rain and hail storm, Clark refreshed the men with a drink of grog. The morning of June 28, Clark had the last remaining canoe and baggage taken to the staging point on the plain. The rest of the items destined for the cache were taken there and buried. Clark wrote "after Covering the *Carshe* & loading the two Carrges with the remaining part of our Baggage we all Set out..." This last trip to White Bear Islands was a struggle. First some of the baggage including kegs of pork and flour had to be left at the staging point on the plain above Belt Creek. The party then proceeded with the carriages to Willow Run where they spent a miserable night due to rain and a cold wind which Clark described as "most dredfull...off the Snow Mountains to the S.W...." The party ate buffalo and drank a dram of grog.

The June 29 weather summary according to Ordway was a little rain in the morning followed by clearing skies and warm temperatures, but then all hell broke loose. Lewis had been so busy with the iron frame canoe he had not seen the Giant Springs, so with Drouillard, he walked overland towards the spring and just as they reached the river breaks, a heavy rain hit and forced the two men to sit "very composedly for about an hour without sheter" and take a "copious drenching of rain...." Clark awoke to find the "Prarie was So wet as to render it impossible to pass on to the end of the portage...." He sent the men back to bring up the baggage which had been left at the staging point, while he, Charbonneau, York, Sacagawea and baby Pomp departed for the great falls. Some of the notes from his survey of June 17 which the wind had blown away during his June 19 walk related to the great falls and Clark wanted to visit them again so he could replace the information. The same violent rain and hailstorm deluged Clark and his party. Upon returning to the Willow Run camp, he found the men in total disarray having been caught in the open plain when the storm hit. Ordway wrote they could see the storm approaching but were unable to reach their camp at Willow Run before it unleashed its fury. To ease the storm's lashing from their memory, Clark dispensed grog to the bruised and battered crew.

The weather improved on June 30 and Clark sent the men in various directions to get all of the tasks completed he wanted done. He wrote, "I dispatch the party except 5 for the remaining baggage Scattered in the plains, two to hunt for meat, two to the falls, and one to Cook at 10 oClock the hunters Came in loaded with fat meat, & those were dispatched for the baggage returned with it. I Set 4 men to make new axeltrees & repare the Carrages, others to take the load across the run which had fallen & is about 3 feet water, men Complain of being Swore this day dull and lolling about...." About 11a.m., Clark sent the party to the six-mile stake with a load. The next morning July 1, the party left Willow Run and proceeded to White Bear Islands. The morning of July 2, the men returned to the 6 mile stake for the baggage and brought it to the island camp. The portage was complete.

In celebration of getting the six canoes and baggage around the falls, the cooks prepared a dinner of bacon, beans, suet dumplings and buffalo meat. The Captains gave the men a "drink of sperits, it being the last of our stock." Lewis wrote, "the fiddle was plyed and they danced very merrily untill 9 in the evening when a heavy shower of rain put an end to that part of the amusement tho' they continued their mirth with songs and festive jokes and were extreemly merry untill late at night." The date of this celebration was July 4, 1805.

THE FALLS

Although the portage was completed on July 2, the Expedition remained in the Great Falls area another two weeks. Most of this time was spent assembling the iron frame canoe and making leather clothing. Because many of the men involved in the portage had not seen the falls, several made the most of this time and did some sightseeing. Gass wrote on July 3, "I was so engaged with the boat, that I had not visited the falls. I therefore set out with one of the men to-day for that purpose."

Four of the five falls seen by Lewis and Clark are visible today. They are the Great Falls, Crooked or Horseshoe Falls, Rainbow Falls and Black Eagle Falls. Colter Falls, the lesser of the five is today submerged in the backwater of Rainbow Dam. Five hydroelectric dams, Black Eagle, Rainbow, Cochrane, Ryan and Morony, have been built on this stretch of the river. The spectacular view of millions of gallons of water flowing freely over the falls as it was when Lewis and Clark observed them, is no longer seen today.

Black Eagle Falls got its name from an eagle which for years made her nest on an island below the falls. The Indians of Fort Mandan had told Lewis and Clark about the bird. Lewis described what he saw on June 14, 1805, "in this Island on a Cottonwood tree an Eagle has placed her nest; a more inaccessable spot I beleive she could not have found; for neither man nor beast dare pass those gulphs which seperate her little domain from the shores." During their stay, Lewis and Clark referred to Black Eagle Falls as the "upper pitch."

Lewis called Rainbow Falls the "Beautiful Cascade and handsome falls." In 1872, Thomas P. Roberts, a railroad surveyor, gave it the name Rainbow Falls because the sun's rays are refracted in the mist producing rainbows which dance through the water and mist as it tumbles over the rocks. Of the names given to the falls by Lewis and Clark, only the name "Crooked Falls" has endured. The name Great Falls came from the Indians of Fort Mandan. Paris Gibson named Colter Falls for Private John Colter, a man whom most people recognize for his discovery of the wonders of Yellowstone Park and for the footrace near Three Forks, Montana in which a naked Colter outran several Blackfeet warriors.

Like a master chef, Lewis prepared a feast of words in describing the beauty of the falls of the Missouri. They paint for us a picture of the Virginia native drinking in the scene and struggling to put on paper words from which Jefferson and others could envision what he was seeing: "I now thought that if a skillfull painter had been asked to make a beautifull cascade that he would most probably have pesented the precise immage of this one; nor could I for some time determine on which of those great cataracts to bestoe the palm, on this or that which I had discovered yesterday; at length I determined between these two great rivals for glory that this was *pleasingly beautiful*, while the other was *sublimely grand*."

WHITE BEAR ISLANDS

On June 18, during his survey of the portage route, Clark reached the location the explorers called White Bear Islands. After looking over the area, Clark settled on these islands as the ending point of the portage. He wrote of the three islands, "passed Some timber in a point at 2 mile at or near the lower point of a large Island on which we Shot at a large white bear.   passed a Small Island in the middle and one close on the Lard Shore at 3 miles behind the head of which we Camped." Later that same day, a grizzly bear chased Willard and very nearly caught him, and after giving up on Willard, the enraged animal turned its attention to Colter and chased him into the water. The bear retreated to the thick bushes of the islands. Clark wrote he could see the bear but could not get a shot at it.

June 21, the evening before the portage started, Lewis "determined to go to the upper part of the portage tomorrow; in order to prepare my boat and receive and take care of the stores as they were transported, I caused the Iron frame of the boat and the necessary tools my private baggage and Instruments to be taken as a part of this load, also baggage of Joseph Fields, Sergt. Gass and John shields, whom I had scelected to assist me in constructing the leather boat." Lewis stayed at the upper camp for the duration of the portage, spending most of his time directing the construction of the iron frame canoe and cooking. Lewis wrote of his boat, "it was a novel piece of machinism to all who are employed my constant attention was necessary to every part of the work; this together with duties of cheif cook has kept me pretty well employed."

White Bear Islands Camp was occupied from June 22 until the morning of July 13. This camp was the spot where these men who had reached so deep into their physical being to get all of the Expedition's goods portaged and ready for the water again, celebrated late into the night of July 4, drinking the last of the grog, singing and dancing to the music of Cruzatte's violin. This camp was also the spot where Lewis experienced one of his most disappointing moments of the entire Expedition when after all of the planning and work, his favorite project the iron canoe failed. And in 1806 when the White Bear Islands cache was opened, Lewis found that all of his patience and hard work collecting plants from Mandan to the falls was for naught. Water had seeped into the hole and destroyed the collection. Jefferson would never be able to examine the specimens.

The islands no longer exist as they did during the time of Lewis and Clark. Of the three, only one is readily distinguishable today. The other two have melded with the river's bank.

WILLOW RUN

On June 16, the two men whom Clark had sent to explore the south side of the river for portage opportunities, returned with the report the country was "unfavourable" due to "the Creek & 2 deep reveens." The second of these ravines acquired its Lewis and Clark name during the first portage trip to White Bear Islands, when "sweet willow" from the area was used to repair the carriages. The willow being a more supple and stronger wood answered the repair needs of the men.

ENGLISH

Today, the Expedition's Willow Run or Willow Creek is known as Box Elder Creek which drains into the Missouri six miles above Belt Creek. During the portage, it was a convenient place about midway on the journey to White Bear Islands where the men could be refreshed. Clark described it as a source of "plenty of fine water and a little wood."

The portage route crossed the prairie some distance from the Missouri, thus water was a concern for the men. On June 24, Ordway described how this problem could be solved by an afternoon rain storm. He wrote "a volent Shower arose from the N.W. hard thunder caught us in a verry hard rain So that in a fiew minutes the ground was covered with water. So that we got a hearty a hearty drink of water in the holes & puddles & C."

Two days later, the weather did not cooperate and the men proceeded on without "puddle water." They arrived thirsty and exhausted at White Bear Islands. Lewis wrote "Whitehouse one of them much heated and fortiegued on his arrivall dank a very hearty draught of water and was taken almost instanly extreemly ill. his pulse were very full and I therefore bled him plentifully from which he felt great relief. I had no other instrument with which to perform this opperation but my pen knife, however it answered very well." Using far fewer words, Whitehouse simply wrote: "I took sick this evening I expect by drinking too much water when I was hot.   I got bled &c."

On June 28, Clark and his portage crew camped at Willow Run, and it was here on the next day the men regrouped after the violent hailstorm that caught them on the open plain. On the 27th, Ordway managed to use some overhanging rocks at the mouth of Willow Run to escape the brunt of a storm. He wrote: "I got under a Shelving rock on one Side of the creek where a[I] kept dry through the hardest of it....the creek rose So high in a fiew minutes that I had to move from the dry place and proceeded on. the wind blew So high that the hail cut verry hard against me and I could hardly keep my feet." But the most exciting event to happen at Willow Run during the Lewis and Clark stay was McNeal's encounter with a grizzly bear in 1806.

SULPHUR SPRING

This spring is located a few hundred yards from the west bank of the Missouri River just opposite the mouth of Belt Creek. The first mention of the spring by any of the journalists is on June 16 when Lewis compared its water to that of Bowyer's Spring in Virginia. It is likely that Joseph Field, the young man who carried Lewis' letter written to Clark telling him the great falls had been found, first saw the spring and told the Captains about it. Lewis would have seen it when he walked on June 16 from the great falls to meet Clark. It is not clear from the journals if Clark ever visited the spring. Whitehouse wrote "the water having a strong sulphurous taste, Our party drank a considerable quantity of this water for their healths which had the desired effect...."

When the Expedition arrived at Belt Creek, Sacagawea had been seriously ill for a number of days. Lewis wrote on June 16 "her pulse were scarcely perceptible, very quick frequently irregular and attended with strong nervous symptoms, that of the twitching of the fingers and leaders of the arm...." He applied poultices of barks and laudanum (tincture of opium), and had a cask of water from the sulphur spring brought to the young mother. He wrote of it, "the water is as transparent as possible strongly impregnated with sulfur, and I suspect Iron also...." He continued, "the virtues of which I now resolved to try on the Indian woman."

Sacagawea drank the water. The next morning, she was improved to the point where she asked for food. Several times during her illness, Clark had bled Sacagawea. This perhaps brought on dehydration, in which case, the mineral water from the spring may have saved the Shoshoni woman's life.

Today, the spring is accessible by walking about two miles downstream along the Missouri River starting from just above Morony Dam. The area and the spring are much the same as when Lewis and Clark were in the area and are a wonderful place to experience a small piece of the trail just as it was in 1805.

THE LEATHER BOAT

Before the Lewis and Clark Expedition, it was generally believed the Missouri and Columbia Rivers had their headwaters in a single chain of mountains running north and south across the continent. The Missouri River ran east from this chain of mountains, the Columbia River ran west. Therefore, it was presumed if one was to travel across the western half of the continent, it would be a matter of navigating up the Missouri, making a portage, perhaps a short portage, across the mountains to the Columbia River and floating down to the Pacific. Jefferson's letter of instructions to Lewis said to follow the Missouri to its headwaters to find the most direct and practicable water communication across the continent. Knowing that there was a chain of mountains to be portaged, Lewis had the Harper's Ferry Arsenal in Virginia build an iron frame which could be covered with hides to form a boat. The frame could easily be portaged over the mountains and then assembled for the river trip to the Pacific.

During 1803 when Lewis was still preparing for the trip, he spent a month at the arsenal. Most of this time he was assisting the workers in preparing the frame. In a letter dated April 20, 1803, Lewis relayed to Jefferson "My detention at Harper's Ferry was unavoidable for one month, period much greater than could reasonably have been calculated on; my greatest difficulty was the frame of the canoe, which could not be completed without my personal attention to such portion of it as would enable the workmen to understand the design perfectly...." He continued in the letter that he ran an experiment using two sections, one curved for the stem/stern and one for the body of the canoe. He spent so much time there the President felt obliged to write him a letter effecting disappointment that the long delay of a month may end up costing a year's time.

Jefferson was certainly informed of the speculation that a portage had to be made across the mountains from one river to the other. It therefore seems reasonable that Jefferson had a hand in the idea for such a watercraft and indeed may have helped Lewis design it. This is certainly the type of project the tinkering president would have delighted in.

Because it was impractical to portage the white pirogue around the falls, Lewis decided to assemble his "experiment," as he called the iron canoe, to take its place. He had anticipated the possibility of not being able to portage the pirogues from the time the Indians of the Mandan area had talked about the portage and had been gathering hides long before the Expedition arrived at the falls. At the White Bear Islands Camp, under the close direction of Captain Lewis, work began on the iron canoe on June 23. When finished, twenty-eight elk skins and four buffalo hides were stretched over the wood and iron frame, 36 feet long, 4 feet 6 inches wide and 26 inches deep with a carrying capacity of 8,000 pounds. Limbs of willow and box elder trees were used as braces. The buffalo hides were singed leaving some hair, whereas the elk hides were shaved. Lewis perceived very early in the project that sealing the seams where the hides were sewn together could be a problem. He wrote, "perceive several difficulties in preparing the leather boat...." One of them was "pitch to pay her seams." These words were written June 21 as Lewis was examining the frame at Lower Portage Camp. There is reason to speculate about why Lewis proceeded with assembling the canoe when he had such well-founded doubts. Maybe it was a matter of determination and the expected satisfaction.

They attempted to make tar to cover the seams, but, as Lewis noted, "our tar-kiln which ought to have began to run this morning has yealded no tar as yet and I am much affraid will not yeald any...."

Unable to come up with pitch in this virtually treeless plain, Lewis mixed up a concoction of beeswax, charcoal and tallow to put on the seams. On July 9, the canoes were loaded and the iron boat launched. He said "she lay like a perfect cork on the water." However, it soon became obvious the seams were leaking and Lewis' experiment would not meet the Expedition's needs. Lewis' words, "I need not add that this circumstance mortifyed me not a little" expressed his wrenching disappointment. Surely the Captain's stomach was twisted into a knot as he continued, "I am preswaided, that had I formed her with buffaloe skins singed not quite as close as I had done those I employed, that she would have answered even with this composition. but to make any further experiments in our present situation seemed to me madness...I therefore relinquished all further hope of my favorite boat and ordered her to be sunk in the water, that the skins might become soft in order the better to take her peices tomorrow and deposit the iron frame at this place as it could be of no further service to us."

If Lewis' original idea was to use this canoe in the mountains where there they would have found plenty of pitch-producing trees, then the question: Why didn't he take it with him to be used once the party reached the great river to the Pacific? is a reasonable question. Maybe the most obvious answer is the Indians had told them there would be no animals in the mountains, so there would be no way to get hides to cover it. Or maybe the Captain was so disgusted he just did not want to try again.

Whether or not Clark was part of the decision to assemble the iron frame canoe at the falls will never be known. How he felt about the project is also unknown. There is probably little doubt Clark may have been concerned about the amount of time and effort it cost the party, especially during the best travel time of the year. When the leather canoe failed in front of the assembled party, it had to have been a trying moment for Captain Lewis. He probably heard the whispers of the men as they talked about their leader's decision to experiment with such an idea. Clark simply wrote "this falire of our favourite boat was a great disappointment to us, we haveing more baggage than our Canoes would Carry." This was written July 9, 1805.

The iron frame was cached at White Bear Islands. It was dug up a year later and Lewis noted it "had not suffered materially." This is the last mention of the iron-frame canoe. What happened to it? Did they take the frame with them or did they toss it back in the cache hole or did Lewis drag it to the river in disgust for a watery burial? With metal being an important trade item, most likely it went down river with Ordway's party. After all, they pulled nails from the red pirogue at the mouth of the Marias and from the canoe left on the Jefferson River. Metal was too valuable to be left behind.

DOG OF THE NEWFOUNDLAND BREED

In 1913, grandsons of Nicholas Biddle, first editor of the Lewis and Clark journals, were preparing to send the papers of their grandfather to the Library of Congress. In sifting through them, one of the boys found the long lost journal of Sergeant John Ordway which eventually was edited by Milo Milton Quaife. As Quaife was reviewing the material from the Biddle boys, he found another journal one which began August 30, 1803. There was a moment of wonderment as to the identity of the journalist. But it was soon clear to Quaife he had found the journal kept by Lewis as the Captain moved the supplies down the Ohio and Mississippi Rivers to eventually set up camp near the mouth of the Missouri. This journal contained the first words written by Lewis as part of the Corps of Volunteers for Northwestern Discovery. It was a huge find in the history of the Lewis and Clark Expedition. No one had any idea Lewis had kept a journal during this time and no one knew until one hundred years after the Expedition that Lewis had purchased a big black Newfoundland dog to take along on the Expedition.

The first mention of Lewis' dog in the Ohio River journal is dated September 11, 1803. Lewis wrote: "observed a number of squirrels swiming the Ohio and universally passing from the W. to the East shore....I made my dog take as many each day as I had occation for, they wer fat and I thought them when fryed a pleasant food.....my dog was of the newfoundland breed very active strong and docile, he would take the squirel in the water kill them and swiming bring them in his mouth to the boat."

In November as Lewis' party passed the Mississippi River, the Captain noted some Indians approached him and one of them offered three beaver skins for the dog. Lewis wrote he was pleased with the qualifications of the newfoundland and "of course there was no bargan, I had given 20$ for this dogg...."

The Lewis and Clark journalists infrequently recorded anything of the dog. Clark wrote in late August 1804 that as several members of the party walked to Spirit Mound in north central South Dakota, the dog gave out and had to be sent back to a creek. When the Expedition was in the mountains dealing with the Shoshoni Indians, Lewis related the Indians were taken with the "segacity of my dog...." In April 1806, as the Expedition was working its way up the Columbia, Indians stole the animal. Lewis ordered three men to pursue the Indians "with orders if they made the least resistence or difficulty in surrendering the dog to fire on them; they overtook these fellows or reather came within sight of them at the distance of about 2 miles; the indians discovering the party in pursuit of them left the dog and fled."

Lewis did not use a formal name for the dog, he preferred to call it "my dog." Ordway, however, recorded the dog's name several times. On July 14, 1804, Ordway wrote Clark and Drouillard shot at some elk and Seamon swam across the river after them. On April 18, 1805, Ordway recorded in his journal "one man killed another goose   Seamon b.out...." May 19, 1805, Ordway wrote "Semon Capt. Lewiss dog got bit by a beaver." These quotations are from the Moulton edition of the Ordway journal and show Ordway always, according to Moulton's interpretation spelled the dog's name with "mon."

Quaife interpreted Ordway's handwriting much differently than did Moulton. On July 14, 1804, Ordway according to Quaife wrote Shannon swam after the elk. On April 18, 1805, the words are "one man killed another goose Scannon b. out." The entry on April 26, Quaife interpreted as "Saw a flock of Goats Swimming the river this morning near to our camp. Cap Lewises dog Scamon took after them [and] caught one in the River." The May 19, 1804 entry is "Semon Cap Lewiss dog got bit by a beaver." May 8, 1806, entry is "Several of the hunters went out and killed 4 Deer one of the hunters wounded a deer only broke its leg Cap Lewises dog Scamon chased it caught it [and] killed it." In Quaife's index, the dog is entitled Scannon (Scamon). So with Milo Milton Quaife's interpretation of Ordway's handwriting, the spelling of the dog's name was: Shannon, Scannon, Scamon, Semon. With Gary Moulton's interpretation of Ordway's handwriting, there is only one spelling: Seamon.

Ernest Staples Osgood, the editor of Clark's Field Notes, called the dog Scannon. On July 5,1804, Osgood's interpretation is: "we came to for Dinner at a Beever house, Cap Lewis's Dog (Scannon) went in & drove them out." In the Summer 1976 edition of the *Montana The Magazine of Western History,* Osgood offered an explanation of how the dog got its name. He wrote: "In the journals he is always called 'my dog,' 'the dog,' 'our dog' or 'Captain Lewises dog.' Nevertheless, he was full grown when his master purchased him and undoubtedly had a name to which he responded. Whatever the reason for this omission may have been, we can thank Sergeant Ordway, a member of the party, for letting us know that 'our dog' really had a name. In an entry in his journal, April 18, 1805, a year and a half after Scannon left Pittsburgh, Ordway wrote, 'One man killed another goose and Scannon brought him out.'"

Clark lists the dog's name on two of his maps and in both instances, it appears to be spelled "Seamon." He also used the same spelling in his list of streams.

So, for many years, we called the big black Newfoundland "Scannon." Then Donald Jackson, the brilliant Lewis and Clark scholar of the 1960's, proposed a name change for the dog. Jackson was working on a piece related to the place names left behind by the Expedition. Most Lewis and Clark place names came from a member of the Expedition, an incident or on rare occasions a friend or dignitary back home. The Judith River was named after Julia Hancock, a young lady Clark would marry January 5, 1808; the Shields River after John Shields; Onion Island because of all the onions found there; and so on. But Jackson could not come up with a reason for the name of Seaman's Creek (today's Monture Creek) which runs into the Blackfoot River in Montana. Finally, Jackson concluded Seaman's Creek was named for Lewis' dog, and Quaife and Osgood were in error when they called the dog "Scannon." Jackson was convinced the dog's name was Seaman. But if we use Moulton's interpretation of the handwriting of Ordway and as Quaife also did, the name of the dog should be Seamon, not Seaman. For Ordway who attempted to spell the name as it sounded to him, it came out Seamon. Taking one more speculative step, it may be the dog's name was Simon, but pronounced as if it were Spanish or French: Simon (see-mon or sea-mon).

Whatever the dog's name, the last known mention of it was in north central Montana as the Expedition passed through the Great Falls area homeward bound. The mosquitoes were relentless in their attack on the party and Lewis wrote, "my dog even howls with the torture he experiences from them...." It is reasonable to think the Newfoundland was there when the party landed in St. Louis. If it had died or been killed, surely one of the journalists would have penned a few words about what happened.

HUGH McNEAL
AND THE CACHES

Lewis and Clark started the Expedition with an estimated 3,500 pounds of supplies and on several occasions lessened their burden by depositing items along the way. This was done with the idea things left would be retrieved on the return trip. Not unlike modern day travelers, some of the items were things collected en route either by the captains or by the men. As the Expedition left Canoe Camp on July 15, 1805, Lewis wrote, "our vessels eight in number all heavily laden, notwithstanding our several deposits...we find it extreemly difficult to keep the baggage of many of our men within reasonable bounds...."

Items were left behind at the mouth of the Marias River, Lower Portage Camp near Belt Creek and at White Bear Islands. In most cases, the items were put into caches made by digging a hole with a top narrower than the bottom. The hole was lined with rocks and branches, and the original sod from the opening was replaced to conceal the location. Dirt from the hole was carefully removed from the area so passers-by were unaware of any disturbance. Lewis recorded that Cruzatte had dug caches before and he was therefore put in charge of preparing the hole and depositing the items.

At the Marias River, they made three deposits. Included in the items left there were "2 best falling axes, one auger, a set of plains, some files, blacksmiths bellowses and hammers Stake tongs &c. 1Keg of flour, 2 Kegs of parched meal, 2 Kegs of Pork, 1 Keg of salt, some chissels, a cooper's Howel, some tin cups, 2 Musquets, 3 brown bear skins, beaver skins, horns of the bighorned anamal, a part of the men's robes clothing and all their superfluous baggage of every description, and beaver traps."

Ordway noted in his journal before they left the Marias on the morning of June 12, they had to bury three traps that had been mistakenly left out of the cache. Whitehouse wrote, "others employed digging another hole So that we might bury in different places what we left So that if the Savages Should find one perhaps they would not find the other & we would have Some left Still." Interestingly the next summer, they could not find the traps; otherwise though, the rest of the items were in fine shape except for the beaver skins and robes which had spoiled.

At Lower Portage Camp, one cache was made. Items left there included: kegs of flour and pork, two blunderbusses, and Captain Lewis' desk. Before this cache was completed, Ordway and another member of the Expedition sought shelter from a threatening rain cloud in it. It was June 27 when he returned from Willow Run to Lower Portage Camp and the sky promised more rain. He wrote, "look likely for more rain. So I and one man more went and Slept in the carsh a hole which was dug to deposit Some baggage...."

On the return trip in 1806, Lewis sent McNeal on horseback to the Lower Portage Camp cache. What started out as a special assignment left McNeal by the end of the day wondering if he would see the sun rise in the morning.

On the way, the Pennsylvania-born man surprised a grizzly bear at Willow Run. Lewis described what happened: "the horse took the allarm and turning short threw him immediately under the bear; this animal raised himself on his hinder feet for battle, and gave him time to recover from his fall which he did in an instant and with his clubbed musquet he struck the bear over the head and cut him with the guard of the gun and broke off the breech, the bear stunned with the stroke fell to the ground and began to scratch his head with his feet; this gave McNeal time to climb a willow tree which was near at hand...." McNeal managed to get up the tree before the bear could recover. The bear however would not admit defeat so easily. It "waited at the foot of the tree untill late in the evening before he left him, when McNeal ventured down and caught his horse which had by this time strayed off to a distance of 2 ms...." For Hugh McNeal, this had to be a front-page story. A story he repeated often and perhaps embellished a bit for the friends and family back home.

Included in the items left at White Bear Islands in 1805 were Lewis' plant specimens he had collected from Fort Mandan to the falls, the iron frame and the truck wheels. Unfortunately, many of the items including the plant collection were destroyed when water got into the cache.

GREAT FALLS GULLY WASHER

Several times during their stay in the Great Falls area, Expedition members were subjected to severe weather conditions. The storm of June 29, 1805 nearly claimed the lives of Clark, Sacagawea and her baby. The same storm left the portage crew scrambling for shelter as hail battered them on the open plains.

Clark and his party of four (Charbonneau, Sacagawea, Pomp, York) had journeyed to the great falls to replace some notes Clark had lost to the wind on June 19. He wrote: "Soon after I arrived at the falls, I perceived a Cloud which appeared black and threaten imediate rain....about 1/4 of a mile above the falls I obsd a Deep rivein in which was Shelveing rocks under which we took Shelter...the rain fell like one voley of water falling from the heavens and gave us time only to get out of the way of a torrent of water which was Poreing down the hill in the rivin with emence force tareing every thing before it takeing with it large rocks & mud...." Clark managed to push Sacagawea and Pomp up the gully wall just in time to avoid being swept away with the flash flood waters as they gushed through the ravine. Clark wrote "the bottom of the revein which was a flat dry rock when I entered it, the water was up to my waste & wet my watch, I Scrcely got out before it raised 10 feet deep with a torrent which turrouble to behold, and by the time I reached the top of the hill, at least 15 feet...." Clark called this coulee "Defeated Drain" on several of his detailed maps of the falls area.

After the storm, Clark wrote they were wet and cold, and he feared the Indian woman, who was just recovering from her illness, would suffer a relapse. He made Sacagawea take a little spirits which York had in a canteen. This revived her very much. He then hurried the party back to the camp at Willow Run where they could get a change of clothes for the baby.

The next morning, Clark sent two men to the ravine to look for the items lost to the sweeping waters. Of those items—including a shot pouch and horn, elegant fusee, umbrella, tomahawk, large surveying compass and the child's cradleboard—only the compass was recovered. This compass was the single one of its type which Lewis and Clark had along and it was needed for their astronomical observations as well as for taking the course of the river. It was extremely fortunate that it was recovered.

As for the men caught in the same storm, Ordway wrote: "ran in great confusion to Camp the hail being So large and the wind So high and violent in the plains, and we being naked we were much bruuzed by the large hail. Some nearly killed one knocked down three times, and others without hats or any thing about their heads bleeding and complained verry much." According to Whitehouse, who was with Lewis at White Bear Islands Camp during the storm, the hail was "amazeing large." He wrote, "we measured & weighed Some of them, and Capt. Lewis made a bowl of Ice punch of one of them they were 7 Inches in Surcumference and weighted 3 ounces." For the Expedition, the only good part of June 29, turned out to be the dram of grog issued by the Captains and the hot soup prepared by the cooks for the evening meal.

CANOE CAMP

Throughout the twenty-eight months of the Expedition, the two Captains never considered abandoning their assignment. The words of Thomas Jefferson "and you are appointed to carry them into execution" were like the scarlet letter, there was no doubt about the direction to proceed. So on July 9, as Clark watched the concoction slip from the seams of the Experiment, there was no whining or complaining about his fellow Captain's judgement, he simply wrote "Concluded to build Canoes for to Carry them; no timber near our Camp. I deturmined to proceed on up the river to a bottom in which our hunters reported was large Trees &c."

It was now early July. Uncertainty about what lay ahead, how far it was to the dividing mountains, how rough the mountains were which they had to pass, and what faced them once they crossed the mountains, caused the Captains to be anxious about their situation. Both realized that success depended on finding the Shoshoni Indians and getting horses to cross the mountains before the white blanket came. There was no longer any thought given to reaching the Pacific and returning to this side of the mountains during the present season. Both men knew time was a precious commodity and they had already wasted too much of it on the iron canoe.

At this point, the Expedition had six canoes, but baggage enough to fill eight. The prospect of finding trees large enough to make canoes was not good in the immediate Great Falls area. The hunters had ranged several miles above White Bear Islands and reported to the Captains that a stand of fairly good-sized cottonwoods grew north of the river. Remembering that the only tree of any size in this area had been used for the carriage wheels,

Lewis wrote, "if we find trees at the place mentioned sufficiently large for our purposes it will be extreemly fortunate."

Plans were made. Clark and eight men were to proceed immediately to the area upstream in hopes of finding trees to suit their purpose. Clark's crew consisted of "Sergt. Pryor four Choppers two Involids & one man to hunt..."

Clark's journal entry for July 10 described the luck they had in finding two suitable trees. He was on the north side of the river and by his estimation about eight land miles from White Bear Islands Camp. He wrote: "found two Trees which I thought would make Canoes, had them fallen, one of them proved to be hollow & split at one End & verry much win Shaken at the other, the other much win Shaken, we Serched the bottoms for better trees and made a trial of Several which proved to be more indifferent. I deturmined to make Canoes out of the two first trees we had fallen, to Contract thir length so as to clear the hollow & winshakes, & ad to the width as much as the tree would allow."

During the next five days, the choppers worked steadily, molding the less-than-ideal cottonwoods into river-ready canoes, battling "Musquitors emencely noumerous & troublesome," and ax handles that repeatedly broke. Clark wrote: "we ar much at a loss for wood to make ax hilthes (handles), 13 hath been made & broken in this piece of a day by the four Choppers, no other wood but Cotton Box elder Choke Cherry and red arrow wood. we Substitute the Cherry in place of Hickory for ax hilthes ram rods, &c. &c"

Throughout the work on the canoes, the captains remained concerned about the time. Lewis wrote on July 12, "I feel excessively anxious to be moving on."

From the 10th to the 15th, the Expedition was split between the White Bear Islands Camp and Canoe Camp. Clark was at Canoe Camp, while Lewis and most of the baggage remained at White Bear Islands. To be ready to proceed just as soon as the two canoes were finished, Sergeant Ordway was charged with moving all of the baggage by canoe to Canoe Camp.

According to Ordway, it was only five miles by land to where Clark's men were hollowing out the trees, but it was twenty by water. The strong prairie winds proved to be almost as formidable in negotiating this stretch of the river as the falls had been below. Ordway and his crew were grounded on several occasions by high winds. On July 10, four canoes set out from the White Bear Islands. One of the canoes carried the baggage and tools of the men assigned to go with Clark. The wind forced them to shore after five or six miles. While they waited for the wind to abate, Whitehouse wrote he walked in the plains and "trod on a verry large rattle Snake." He described the snake as being 4 feet 2 inches long and 5 1/2 inches around. He wrote "it bit my leggin on my legg I shot it."

Ordway wrote, "late in the afternoon the wind abated a little So we proceeded on within about 3 miles of the upper Camp [Canoe Camp]...." The next day, the wind again blew very hard and three of the canoes were grounded until evening of July 11. Finally, the men managed to get the one canoe carrying the tools to Clark.

Pryor, who had been taken along to provide meat for the men working on the canoes, dislocated his shoulder. It was manipulated into place, but not without considerable pain. This would not be the last time the cousin of the only man to die while on the Expedition would suffer with shoulder problems. Bratton suffered from an infected finger and could not wield an ax, so he was told to return on foot to White Bear Islands for tools.

Once the other canoes arrived they were unloaded, and three of them were immediately sent back. However, the wind was so strong during the night they did not make Lewis' camp until noon on the 12th. Ordway wrote, "the wind rose So high that one canoe filled with water the other 2 took in water the waves high but with difficulty we got down to Camp about noon."

On the 13th, the Expedition finally abandoned the White Bear Islands Camp. After crossing the Missouri by canoe, Lewis, Sacagawea and Lepage walked over land to Canoe Camp. The rest of the party with the remaining baggage traveled by canoe. On the way, Lewis came across a "very extraordinary Indian lodge," which was 216 feet in circumference and was made with sixteen cottonwood poles each fifty feet long. This structure was most likely a medicine lodge constructed by the Blackfeet Indians as part of their sundance ritual.

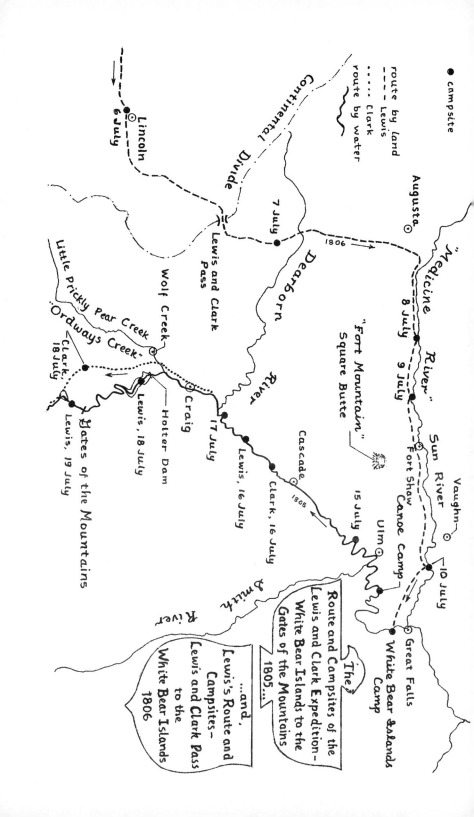

TO THE GATES OF THE MOUNTAINS

On July 15, more than a month from the time Lewis first arrived at the falls, the Expedition was finally ready to depart the area. He wrote, "We arrose very early this morning assigned the canoes their loads....we now found our vessels eight in number all heavily laden, notwithstanding our several deposits; tho' it is true we have now a considerable stock of dryed meat and grease." In fact their canoes were so full, that several of the men, including both Captains, had to walk.

Lewis continued, "At 10 A.M. we once more saw ourselves fairly under way much to my joy and I beleive that of every individul who compose the party." Clark was not given to discussing how the party felt at the moment. He wrote that it rained all night and he got wet, very wet. Lewis felt a sense of accomplishment and relief. The great falls of the Missouri, all five of them, were fading pictures in the back of his mind. They had wrestled with nature's road block, survived a violent pounding with hail stones as big as baseballs, frolicked daily with the unneighborly grizzly bears, pulled enough prickly pear spines from their feet to stake a claim in the Oklahoma land rush, swallowed the last drop of their liquor and lamented about leaving the beautiful plains where, every day, it was just a matter of killing elk, deer, buffalo, antelope to prepare a feast that would have pleased the friends and relatives back home who were now wondering if they might already be dead.

In the days before the Expedition moved up river, Lewis had walked along the rocky ridges north and west of Canoe Camp. He took the bearings of three chains of mountains and a flat-topped butte he labeled Fort Mountain (Square Butte). A hundred years later, Charles M. Russell put this same curious geologic work of nature into his magnificent oil painting "When the Land Belonged To God."

During the next couple of days, the Missouri River took them on a back-and-forth accordion path that must have left the men shaking their heads about so much effort for so few degrees of longitude. From the Great Falls to the Three Forks, most of the miles traveled were south, much fewer were west. The Expedition passed a river entering the Missouri a few miles east of Ulm, Montana. It was named Smith River after Robert Smith, Secretary of the Navy during Jefferson's Administration. Just after they passed the Smith, Drouillard wounded a deer which ran into the river. Lewis wrote, "my dog pursued caught it drowned it and brought it to shore at our camp."

The sunflower was just starting to bloom in the river bottoms and Lewis wrote about how much he liked the Indian recipe for making a kind of dough from the seeds. After parching the seeds, the Indians pounded them into a fine powder which was mixed with water and marrow grease to make a dough. Lewis thought it was very "pallateable" and he had a hearty appetite for it. Any food made from seeds or berries was a welcome change for the men whose diet mainstay was protein. Lewis estimated that it took four deer, or a deer and an elk, or one buffalo to supply them with food for a twenty-four hour period.

July and early August is the time when the prickly pear cacti put forth some of the most beautiful blossoms in all of nature. Lewis wrote it is one of the great beauties of the plains, but he reminded his readers in the same sentence, that it is also one of the "greatest pests of the plains."

After an early start on July 16, the Expedition passed "little booths" which had been prepared by Indians presumed to be the Shoshoni Indians. It was an encouraging sign for the party. A buffalo was shot for breakfast, and Lewis wrote for the first time that the small guts were prepared Indian style and he found them very good. The Indian recipe was simple: do not wash or clean them, just cook them over a blazing fire. Ordway likely had a keen appetite because he had been instructed to return down river to look for an ax which Lewis wrote he had "carelessly" left behind.

After breakfast, Lewis, Potts, Lepage and Drouillard walked over land on the starboard or northwest side of the river through the area where Cascade, Montana is located. They continued along the high rock walls bordering this section of the river. Lewis wrote about a large rock formation presiding over a gap formed by the river at his camp. He climbed the rock, washed on one side by the river, and bordered on the other three sides by a handsome plain, and from its top, he had a good view of the country through which they had just passed. Lewis and his party spent the night near this rock which he called "the tower." The Captain had forgotten his netting and was an easy target for the swarms of mosquitoes. He was most unhappy with himself and wrote, "promised in my wrath that I never will be guily of similar peice of negligence on this voyage."

Near Lewis' Tower Rock, there is a rapid (Pine Rapid, Pine Island Rapid, today Halfbreed Rapids) which promised difficulty in getting the canoes around it. Taking no chances, Lewis noted he had his box of instruments removed from the canoe and hand carried around the rough water. The "Tower Rock" is just south of Hardy, Montana. The old highway (US 91) ran to the west of it; whereas the interstate cuts across its eastern side. The Missouri once flowed west of this rock and cut the valley there before changing to its present location.

On July 18, they passed a considerable river running into the Missouri from the northwest. Lewis wrote that "this handsome bold and clear stream we named in honor of the Secretary of War, Henry Dearborn, calling it Dearborn's river."

Once Lewis and Clark had successfully negotiated their way around the falls of the Missouri, their next major concern was the mountains separating them from the Columbia River. The Shoshoni Indians held the key to the mountain passage so, shortly after the Expedition departed the Great Falls area, Lewis and Clark became anxious to meet with them. When they passed the Dearborn River it was decided that Clark should lead a party (Potts, York, and Joseph Field) overland to search for the Shoshoni. Clark reasoned "we thought it prudent for a partey to go a head for fear our fireing Should allarm the Indians...." Clark followed the river to a point just downstream from Holter Dam where he turned south on an Indian road and, in doing so, circled west around the Gates of the Mountains.

Lewis and the main party continued up river twenty-one miles. During the evening, they passed a large creek on the north side of the Missouri, naming it for Sergeant Ordway. Unfortunately, this name was unknown by those who came later and it was renamed Little Prickly Pear Creek. Each day as the party passed through the sheer rock walls of this stretch of the river, they saw herds of big horn sheep. Lewis was amazed at their agility and wrote they "bounded from rock to rock with apparent uncon-cern...."

The sheer rock walls of the Gates of the Mountains were not a welcome sight to Lewis. On July 19, he wrote, "every object here wears a dark and gloomy aspect. the tow[er]ing and pro-jecting rocks in many places seem ready to tumble on us." He continued: "the river appears to have woarn a passage just the width of it's channel or 150 yds. it is deep from side to side nor is ther in the 1st 3 miles of this distance a spot except one of a few yards in extent on which a man could rest the soal of his foot." The party was forced to continue on until after dark be-fore they finally found a place large enough to accommodate them for the night. Lewis wrote "from the singular appearance of this place I called it the *gates of the rocky mountains*."

Although Holter Dam has raised the level of the water in the narrow canyon where Lewis' Gates of the Mountains are lo-cated, it is still a spot on the Lewis and Clark Trail where visitors can, with few modern interruptions sense the country much the same way Lewis did in 1805. Many have written that Lewis' words "dark and gloomy" indicate the steep rocky walls put the Captain in a depressed mood. Perhaps. But we must remember that it was late in the evening when they entered and nearly dark before they found a place to camp. It would have been a gloomy prospect for most.

Almost 150 years after Lewis' Expedition struggled to find a place to camp where there was room for only the "soal of the foot," young robust smoke jumpers from the U.S. Forest Service in Missoula, Montana parachuted into the head of one of the drainages just south of the gates. It was late in the afternoon of August 5, 1949 and, just like Lewis who never considered backing away from Jefferson's assignment, these men jumped from the C-47 plane as it circled into the head of the drainage where smoke was rising from the south ridge confident that by 10 a.m. the next morning the fire would be under control. Today, visitors to Mann Gulch walk up the steep hillside where thirteen white crosses stand to remind us that nature was not to be denied. The fire burned for days. The questions about what happened have haunted visitors for years.

PACK RATS and GRIZZLY BEARS

Thomas Jefferson suspicioned and hoped that Lewis' Expedition might encounter mammoths. They were on Jefferson's list of living animals included in his *Notes on Virginia* and he felt somewhere in some corner of the world, the mammoth still lived. It was part of the belief that species did not become extinct. If fossils were found then the living animal might be found. The American Philosophical Society asked its members to search for skeletons and fossils of rare animals including the mammoth. The letter of instructions which Jefferson drafted for Lewis asked the Captain to observe and record descriptions of all natural things. Lewis followed the President's directive and although he never found a mammoth, he did write descriptions of many species unfamiliar to Jefferson and the members of the American Philosophical Society.

There were a couple weeks in September 1804 when Lewis must have stayed up late every night writing in the light of the campfire about animals he had never seen. It started with the black-tailed prairie dog *(Cynomys ludovicianus)* continued with sharp tailed grouse *(Pediocetes phasianellus)*, the pronghorn *(Antilocapra americana)*, white-tailed jack rabbit *(Lepus townsendii)*, mule deer *(Odocoileus hemionus)*, black-billed magpie *(Pica pica)*, coyote *(Canis latrans)*, and ended with the gray wolf *(Canis lupus)*.

At the mouth of the Marias Lewis mentioned there were narrow and wide leaf plains cottonwood trees *(Populus sargentii)* on the banks of the Teton River. The narrow leaf was new to science. And on the 1806 trip up the Marias, Lewis identified black cottonwood trees *(Populus tricho carpa)* and recognized them as being the same as those on the coast. Of the three species, only the black cottonwood grows west of the continental divide. From the observations he made on his 1805 walk up the Marias, Lewis wrote about seeing brown curlews *(Numenius americanus)*, a lark-like bird (McCown's longspur *Calcarius mccownii*) and a large species of heath hen, the wonderful bird of the short grass plain, the sage grouse *(Centrocercus urophasianus)*. In the falls area, Lewis found speckled, pale-blue eggs laid on the ground without any nesting material. He thought these belonged to the curlew; however, he was in error. The curlew egg is olive colored with brownish-colored spots.

During the walk in search of the falls, Goodrich, who could out fish all others on the Expedition, caught three species of fish new to science. The evening of June 11, he caught the sauger and goldeye *(Hiodon alosoides)*. Just two days later, he caught a beautiful trout with splashes of bright red running vertically behind its head. Montana now claims Goodrich's catch, the cutthroat trout, as the state fish. Although Clark was never mentioned as fishing during the entire stint of the Expedition, it still seems appropriate the scientific name of the cutthroat is *Oncorlynchus clarkii*. (Interestingly, the westslope cutthroat is *Oncorhynchus clarki lewisi* and the Yellowstone cutthroat is *O. clarki bouvieri*.)

On the first portage trip, Lewis wrote "there is a kind of larke here that much resembles the bird called the oldfield lark with a yellow brest and a black spot on the croop...." Even the most amateur bird observer recognizes the bird with a black spot on its yellow breast as the western meadowlark *(Sturnella neglecta)*. This prairie bird loves to sit on fence posts and chortle to passersby and, like the cutthroat, was acclaimed as Montana's state symbol. It was a new discovery to science and Lewis should have been given credit for it.

Lewis and Clark experienced a visit from a critter that has over the years developed quite a reputation amongst residents of the plains and mountains of the west. Compared to many cabin dwellers whose damning words echo through the mountain valleys, Clark simply wrote the rat was busy rummaging through the stores of the Expedition and had "done some mischief." Lewis described the new species as a large rat with black eyes, long whiskers and a tail longer than the body and covered with fur. This was the first scientific description of the pack rat *(Neotoma cinerea)*.

In the falls area, there was a small fox which Lewis observed as living in communities and making their homes in burrows in the plains. Today, the swift fox *(Vulpes velox velox)* is rarely seen in Montana. And a couple of days after Lewis wrote his description of the swift fox, he wrote the men brought a live squirrel to camp. Lewis was taken with the little animal and called it "much hadsomer" than those with which he was familiar. Like the kit fox, the thirteen-striped ground squirrel *(Spermophilus tridecemlineatus)* was new to science and is rarely seen in Montana today.

There is limited recorded information about the numbers of passenger pigeons *(Ectopistes migratorius)* in the Rocky Mountain country. Clark and Lewis noted their existence, but the numbers did not compare with the huge flocks which darkened the skies of the east. Clark recorded them as being around camp on July 12, 1805. In 1806 as Lewis' party was returning to the Great Falls area, he wrote they saw pigeons in the area of Lewis and Clark Pass. This simple observation provided information about the western limits of this small dove-like bird which is now extinct. The last wild passenger pigeon was shot March 24, 1900.

By the time the Expedition left the Great Falls area in mid-July 1805, fruits were beginning to appear on the bushes growing along the banks of the river. For Lewis' crew, the currents and gooseberries brought a change in the monotonous diet of meat. On July 17, Lewis wrote "there are a great abundance of red yellow perple & black currants, and service berries now ripe and in great perfection. I find these fruits very pleasant particularly the yellow currant which I think vastly preferable to those of our gardens." Because he knew the President would want to cultivate any new species which might be beneficial to the people of the young democracy, Lewis collected seeds from many plants.

And after several days of sampling the various species of currents, Lewis finally concluded he preferred the black ones.

After they left the Gates of the Mountains, Lewis saw a bird unlike any he had ever seen. He described it as a black woodpecker with a long tail and noted it flew like the jay bird. The next year, he got his hand on one and wrote a description of the bird commonly called Lewis' woodpecker *(Melanerpes lewis)*. Located in the Harvard Museum of Comparative Anatomy is a bedraggled specimen of Lewis' woodpecker, perhaps it is the one from which Lewis wrote his description.

For all of the travel time that the Expedition spent in what is today Montana, it is interesting that there were very few sightings of moose *(Alces alces)* and none were killed. On July 7, 1806, Lewis wrote that Reubin Field wounded a "moos deer," near camp and that the presence of the animal had upset the dog.

Before they departed with the Corps of Discovery, it is likely the young men who were fortunate to be chosen to go on the Expedition had heard the talk on the streets of St. Louis about the grizzly bear. There is little doubt they wanted and expected to meet the bear with a reputation which reached well beyond its home in the west. The first mention of the animal by any Lewis and Clark journalist was October 1, 1804 when a Frenchman told Lewis' crew of white bear being plentiful in the mountains. During the Mandan winter, the Indians told stories of the white bear who, when aggravated, was unbelievably aggressive and strong in pursuit of its tormentors. Lewis found the Indian stories hard to believe. He felt with their modern arms, the bear could not be a match for them. After several encounters with the white bear on the plains of what would become Montana, Lewis had a change of heart and he readily admitted the bear was every bit as bad as the Indians had said it was.

The first specimen of the bear with long neck hairs which glisten white in the sun's rays was taken in northeastern Montana. As the men dressed the young male bear, Lewis penned the first ever scientific notations of the grizzly bear. This was the first of forty-two killed by members of the Lewis and Clark Expedition while in Montana. And while Lewis was busy with the bear, Clark's mind was on a woman whose image must still have been fresh in his memory after more than a year from the time he might have seen her. He called the muddy drainage feeding into the Missouri from the south "Marthys" river. Whoever she was, this woman had made a lasting impression on the thirty-five year old red-haired Captain. People who came later were much less imaginative in their name selection and Martha's River is today called Muddy Creek.

Lewis was familiar with the work of Carolus Linneaus, the great Swedish naturalist whose ideas were the beginning of our modern classification system for all life forms. He had received first-hand training in species classification from Benjamin Smith Barton and had in his baggage Barton's *Elements of Botany*. So when he questioned if the white or yellow bears that the Expedition was encountering on the high plains was a new species and when he wondered if the light-colored bears were different than the grizzly bears, it is understandable. On June 13 the same day he wrote on and on about the falls, Lewis put his thoughts down on paper about the incredible animals:

> "I am induced to believe that the Brown, the white and the Grizly bear of this country are the same species only differing in colour from age or more probably from the same natural cause that many other anamals of the same family differ in colour. one of those which we killed yesterday was of a creemcoloured white while the other in company with it was of the common bey or rdish brown, which seems to be the most usual colour of them. the white one appeared from it's tallons and teath to be the

youngest; it was smaller than the other, and although a monstrous beast we supposed that it had not yet attained it's growth and that it was a little upwards of two years old. the young cubs which we have killed have always been of a brownish white, but none of them as white as that we killed yesterday. one other that we killed sometime since which I mentioned sunk under some driftwood and was lost, had a white stripe or list of about eleven inches wide entirely arround his body just behind the shoalders, and was much darker than these bear usually are. the grizly bear we have never yet seen. I have seen their tallons in possession of the Indians and from their form I am perswaded if there is any difference between this species and the brown or white bear it is very inconsiderable. There is no such anamal as a black bear in this open country or of that species generally denominated the black bear"

His journal entry of February 15, 1806 contains a list of quadrupeds from the Rocky Mountains to the Pacific Ocean. He listed the white, brown or grizzly bears as the same species with variations in color and thought it might be acceptable to call them "the variagated bear." He was right, there is only one species–*Ursus arctos horribilis*. (*Ursus arctos horribilis* is the name now accepted by science, since the Alaska grizzly was named first, and the two are of the same species. The designator "horribilus" thus becomes a "type" or "sub-species.")

Many of Lewis' men returned home with grizzly bear stories. It is reasonable pondering to imagine that when Lewis entered the President's house in December of 1806 and he and Jefferson sat down to talk, that one of the first stories Lewis told the President was about the great white bears. And the men who were fortunate to survive scraps with the animal were most likely telling their stories on the streets of St. Louis on September 24, 1806. One such story would have arisen from the day when Droulliard and Joseph Field were returning to White Bear Island. They discovered bear tracks along the shore and concocted a plot to get the animal. They quietly landed the canoe, climbed a leaning tree, positioned themselves in the branches and then gave a loud hoop. The grizzly appeared instantly and rushed the tree. Drouillard waited just a moment for the bear to stop and then shot it in the head. It turned out to be one of the largest killed by the men of the Expedition. And surely McNeal told and re-told the story of his encounter with the bear at Willow Run.

Grizzly bears found the falls country a good place to live. The islands upstream had considerable cover and the buffalo many of which drowned in the river above and below the falls, provided an easy source of food. The grizzly bears which Lewis and Clark encountered around the falls were some of the best scavengers in the area. There was little need for them to kill anything. Lewis wrote on June 27 that "a bear came within thirty yards of our camp last night and eat up abut thirty weight of buffaloe suit which was hanging on a pole." He went on to say his dog was a good sentinel and alerted the camp of any bear activity.

RETURN TO MONTANA-SUMMER OF 1806

During the winter on the Pacific Coast, Lewis and Clark made plans to explore more of the country known today as Montana. It was decided to send one party down the Yellowstone River, while another party would return to the Great Falls via the "river to the road to the buffaloe [Cokahlarishkit]." Part of the Great Falls group would then proceed down river to the Marias, while Lewis and several of the men would ride horseback into the Marias River country in search of any river draining the rich fur country to the north of 50 degrees of latitude. The Expedition left the coast in March and on June 30, 1806, arrived on the eastern side of the Bitterroot Mountains near Missoula, Montana. Here on July 3, 1806, the two Captains took leave of each other. It was an emotional parting for the two men. Lewis wrote "I took leave of my worthy friend and companion Capt. Clark and the party that accompanyed him. I could not avoid feeling much concern on this occasion although I hoped this seperation was only momentary."

Clark and his party returned to the Three Forks country where he split his group. Sergeant Ordway and nine others returned from there to the Great Falls area in the canoes retrieved from their watery storage at the forks of the Red Rock River and Horse Prairie Creek. The Expedition had sunk them in a pond in the fall of 1805 prior to crossing the mountains. Clark went on horseback through the Gallatin Valley to the Yellowstone River. Clark's party included Sacagawea, Charbonneau and baby Pomp.

On July 7, Lewis and his group of nine rode horseback up Alice Creek to a break in the mountains northeast of Lincoln, Montana. Today this low crossing is called Lewis and Clark Pass. At this point, Lewis crossed the Continental Divide back into the land where the waters drain to the Atlantic Ocean. He had an expansive view of the plains including "Fort Mountain." They then rode in a northerly direction towards the Sun River and camped just east of Table Mountain. During the evening, Drouillard killed two beaver and wounded a third which escaped after inflecting a deep bite to Drouillard's leg. The next morning, they continued north passing Haystack Butte (Shishequaw Mountain). Lewis described this butte as a "high insulated conic mountain." They camped on an island in the Sun River about twenty miles north of State Highway 21. The morning of July 9 was cold and rainy. They spent some time in old Indian lodges, but finally continued on in the rain. Lewis wrote it rained without intermission and they got wet to the skin. Finally he halted the party and made camp near the mouth of Simms Creek. He wrote that they "feasted" on buffalo.

The next day they continued down the Sun River to a point about five miles west of the city of Great Falls. Lewis shot a large white wolf. He wrote it was the "whitest woolf I have seen." Drouillard killed a grizzly bear after it swam the river and another bear gave chase to Gass and Thompson. Being mounted on horseback, the two men were able to out distance the animal.

Clark's summary of the best route from the great falls to Travelers Rest Creek pointed out the big difference in the number of miles between the way the Expedition traveled in 1805 and Lewis' return to the falls in 1806. He wrote: "The most derect and best Course from the dividing ridge which divides the waters of the Columbia from those of the Missouri at the Gap where Capt Lewis crossed it is to leave a Short range of mountains which pass the missouri at the Pine Island rapid to the right passing at it's base and through the plains pass fort mountain to the White bear Isds or medecine river, fine road and about 45 miles, reducing the distance from Clarks river to 145 miles— one other road passses from the enterance of Dearborns River over to a South branch of the Cohahlarishkit river…" After reading this, a question may come to mind. Why did not Lewis and Clark take this route in 1805? Even though the Indians of the Fort Mandan country may have told them of this road, the Expedition had been directed to trace the Missouri to its headwaters and secondly, the Expedition was not at this point prepared to make an overland march. Horses would not be obtained until the Shoshoni were found near Lemhi Pass.

BULL BOATS ON THE UPPER MISSOURI

On July 11, 1806, Lewis and his party of nine (Drouillard, Joseph Field, Reuben Field, Gass, Werner, Frazier, Goodrich, McNeal, Thompson) arrived back at the falls of the Missouri River. It was just one year later almost to the day when they had left this area to proceed on to the western mountains and the Pacific Ocean. Lewis expressed his pleasure in being back in the plains of Montana. He wrote, "the morning was fair and the plains looked beatifull..." After being subjected to a winter-long diet of fish and roots and spoiled elk, the party was appreciative of re-entering the land of the buffalo. On July 9, two days after crossing Lewis and Clark Pass, the party killed a very fat buffalo bull and, Lewis wrote, "we halted to dine."

The first night back at the falls was spent on the west shore just opposite the islands. The men killed eleven buffalo for meat and hides. Lewis planned to leave three men at the falls to help Ordway with the portage and he wanted to leave a supply of meat for the three who were not hunters and might not be able to secure meat for themselves. The next morning July 12, ten of the seventeen horses were missing and Lewis dispatched several men to look for them. Some were found, but in the afternoon, Lewis sent Joseph Field and Drouillard to look for the others. Field returned at dark, but Drouillard did not. The next day July 13 there was no sign of Drouillard and the last words of Lewis' journal on July 14 were: "Drewyer did not return this evening.–" The next day the man who later would be killed by the Blackfeet at the Three Forks returned. From the words of the thirty-two year old Captain we understand how much this half Shawnee-half French man meant to him: "his safe return has releived me from great anxiety. I had already settled it in my mind that a whitebear had killed him and should have set out tomarrow in surch of him...I felt so perfectly satisfyed that he had returned in safety that I thought but little of the horses although they were seven of the best I had."

Because Lewis and his party had arrived at White Bear Islands from the west, it was necessary to construct something to get their baggage across the river to the 1805 campsite. So, they again got into the business of building boats. However, unlike the 1805 task of hollowing out canoes from cottonwood trees, this time the party made bull boats similiar to what they had seen the Indians of Fort Mandan make. Using green buffalo hides with the hair side out, they made two bull boats. Lewis wrote "the one we made after the mandan fassion with a single skin in the form of a bason and the other we constructed of two skins on a plan of our own." Their efforts resulted in two canoes which "answered even beyond our expectations." About 5 pm on July 12 after the wind died down, the baggage was put into the bowl-shaped canoes and transported across the river to White Bear Islands. The July 12, 1806 camp was about a mile below (north) the White Bear Islands camp of 1805. Gass indicated the July 13 camp was moved south to the spot of the 1805 White Bear Islands Camp.

As they had the previous summer, the mosquitoes made life miserable for the men. On the 15th of July, Lewis described their existence with the pesky insects, "the musquetoes continue to infest us in such manner that we can scarcely exist; for my own part I am confined by them to my bier at least 3/4th of my time." He continued "they are almost insupportable, they are so numerous that we frequently get them in our thrats as we breath."

Lewis arrived at the falls with several horses, but after the surreptitious Indian raid, only ten remained. This disrupted Lewis' plans for taking six men to explore the Marias River drainage. It now meant the number traveling north would have to be smaller because some of the horses had to be left at the falls to help with the portage. Lewis' first plan was to leave only Goodrich, McNeal and Thompson at the falls preparing for the portage while the rest rode north and west to see if any branch of the Marias lay as far north as 50 degrees of latitude. Goodrich and McNeal were suffering from the "pox" contracted from the Indian women during the winter on the coast, and Lewis thought that by leaving them at the falls, they would have time to rest and doctor freely with mercury. In the end, Lewis took just three men with him leaving behind Goodrich, McNeal, Thompson, Gass, Frazier and Werner. He wrote, "I have yet 10 horses remaining, two of the best and two of the worst of which I leave to assist the party in taking the canoes and baggage over the portage and take the remaining 6 with me...."

On July 17, Lewis, the two Field brothers and Drouillard set out for the Marias River. Two days later, Ordway and his party swung their six canoes into the bank of White Bear Islands. The plans which Clark and Lewis had decided on during the miserable rainy winter at Fort Clatsop were falling into place.

THE ROAR OF THE BUFFALO

A "tremedious roaring" which Lewis noted could be heard for many miles greeted the Expedition members when they arrived at White Bear Islands. Lewis described the scene: "when I arrived in sight of the whitebear Islands the missouri bottoms on both sides of the river were crouded with buffaloe I sincerely belief that there were not less than 10 thousand buffaloe within a circle of 2 miles...." It was the season of cows with bloody shoulders, and the Expedition horses were not accustomed to the large shaggy beasts and were "much allarmed" at the bellowing of the bulls. Lewis wrote this description on July 11, 1806. On the 13th, he noted, "the buffaloe are leaving us fast and passing on to the S. East." The buffalo were following their annual migration route to fresh grass which for years crossed the Missouri River at the Rock Bottom Crossing, the Indian name for the rocky shelf in the river just downstream from the mouth of the Sun River.

During the time of the Expedition, the plains often appeared to be a moving carpet of dark brown as herds of thousands of buffalo drifted from one grassy area to another. The Lewis and Clark journalists were in awe of the uncountable numbers and they wrote descriptive passages about the buffalo being swept away in the turbulent water as it rushed over the falls. On June 17, 1805, Clark wrote: "I saw 2 herds of those animals watering

immediately above a considerable rapid, they decended by a narrow pass to the bottom Small, the [river] forced those forwd into the water Some of which was taken down in an instant, and Seen no more   others made Shore with difficuelty, I beheld 40 or 50 of those Swimming at the Same time those animals in this way are lost and accounts for the number of buffalow carcases below the rapids."

Lewis said, "their mangled carcases ly along the shores below the falls in considerable quantities and afford fine amusemnt for the bear wolves and birds of prey; this may be one reason and I think not a bad one either that the bear are so tenatious of their right of soil in this neighbourhood."

Eighty-one years later, the *Great Falls Tribune* ran a story about how locals were surprised when they saw thirty head of buffalo in the Sweet Grass Hills. By this time, the buffalo numbers were so few that ten railroad cars could have transported all those remaining across Montana.

1806 PORTAGE OF THE FALLS

July 3, 1806, Clark's party consisted of twenty men and Sacagawea and her baby Pomp. Mounted on horseback, they moved rather quickly through the country from near what is today Missoula, Montana to Camp Fortunate where the canoes had been sunk in a pond. By July 10, the canoes were once again floating on the water of "Jefferson's River" under the direction of Sergeant Ordway. Three days later, the canoe party and the horse party arrived in the Three Forks country. Here Clark and his party of twelve set out for the Yellowstone drainage, while Ordway and his party of nine (Collins, Colter, Cruzatte, Howard, Lepage, Potts, Weiser, Whitehouse and Willard) continued their canoe travel to White Bear Islands arriving there about 3 pm on July 19. Captain Lewis and his horseback party had arrived at the Island's camp on July 11 and Lewis, Drouillard, Joseph and Reubin Field departed horseback on their exploration of the Marias on July 16.

Prior to his departure into the Marias country, Lewis' men dug up the wheels and iron frame of the "Experiment" and the caches at both Upper and Lower Portage Camps. The mosquitoes were relentless in their attack on any exposed flesh. Buffalo dung fires were set and the men and horses huddled downwind of the flames to get some relief in the smoke. Ordway wrote they were worse than last year, and Ordway's party lost no time repairing the wagons and wheels to get them ready for the portage.

The evening of July 20, the four horses were hitched to the carriages for a trial run. Other than the mosquitoes and gnats which covered the horses and the men, Ordway went to sleep that night feeling comfortable that in the morning the first trip to Lower Portage Camp would be completed without incident.

With the appearance of the sun's first rays, one of the men was stirring about camp to get the horses ready for the portage, but the horses were nowhere in sight. Several of the men hunted for them all day knowing full well if they did not find the horses, the ten men would have to pull and push the wagons to Belt Creek just as they had done in reverse the previous year. The men had vivid memories of the exertion required to move the carriages loaded with canoes and gear. Every effort went into finding the two good horses and the two less-than-ideal horses.

Loosing hope they would find them, Ordway had two canoes and some baggage loaded on the carriages and started towards Belt Creek. The party did not get far when Ordway made the decision to delay until tomorrow, hoping somehow they could find the animals. He wrote the morning of July 22 they "rose eairly and turned out in different directions in Search of our 4 horses about noon they were found at the grand falls of Missourie and we tackled up the horses and set out with 2 canoes."

In contrast to the previous summer's portage, the one made in 1806 was not as grueling and demanding. The saddle horses turned work horses got the job done in five days, less than half the time it took in 1805. But, like the 1805 portage, the make-shift carts suffered many break downs. Ordway wrote the first day out, the axeltree broke about five miles from Upper Portage Camp so they left the canoes and baggage under the care of one man and returned to the islands where they made another axeltree. They then started with two more canoes. The next morning, after having camped at the spot where they got the canoes to, they started again. This time the wheels on the carriage carrying the large canoe broke several times. Disgusted, Ordway's crew threw in the towel on the carriage hauling the big canoe. It was decided they could do without the big canoe and it was left on the plain somewhere between White Bear

Islands and Willow Run. Finally near dark, they got two canoes and some of the baggage to Willow Run where they camped. During the day, Wiser suffered a bad knife wound to his leg and had to be transported across the plains in a canoe.

The weather was wet. It rained and hailed during the evening of the 22nd and on the 24th, the clouds delivered another hard shower of rain. The next day, Ordway's crew experienced more rain. He wrote the plains were "So amazeing & bad" they had to hault the portage. July 25, more rain fell and he wrote "we having no Shelter Some of the men and myself turned over a canoe & lay under it others Set up by the fires. the water run under us and the ground was covred with water. the portage River raises fast…" On the morning of July 26, a stray Indian dog showed up in camp and the men fed it.

The men pointed their attention on getting the canoes and gear to Belt Creek. While part of the them returned to Willow Run for the other canoes and baggage, Colter and Potts ran canoes down Belt Creek to the Missouri where the white pirogue was hidden in the bushes. Ordway noted that they had to help the horses pull the carriages because the wheels sank into the rain-soaked plains nearly to the hub. It was with "much hard fatigue" they got the canoes and baggage to where the white pirogue was. But with the beckoning of home, the party wasted no time and, the next morning, after hauling the white pirogue from the bushes and getting it into the Missouri, Ordway's party departed the area about noon. They were headed down the Missouri River in five canoes and the white pirogue. Gass and Willard swam the four horses across the Missouri and headed overland to the Marias. The two parties were to wait for Captain Lewis at the confluence of the Marias and Missouri Rivers. At this point, Lewis' Expedition of thirty-three was separated into five groups in the country that would in 1889 become the State of Montana.

CAMP DISAPPOINTMENT

Lewis, the two Field brothers and Drouillard left White Bear Islands on July 16. To those he left behind at the falls, Lewis gave instructions to join him at the mouth of the Marias. He expected to be there on or before August 5. If this did not happen, Lewis told Gass they should wait until September 1 and then proceed downstream to meet Clark at the mouth of the Yellowstone.

Lewis' final departure of the falls of the Missouri was not as uncomplicated as he might have liked. He had planned to leave on the 15th, but McNeal was using one of the horses he wanted for the Marias River trip. He wrote, "indeed I should have set out instantly but McNeal road one of the horses which I intend to take and has not yet returned." Then the next morning, the horses could not be found until 10 a.m., at which time Lewis wrote, "I immediately set out."

Being camped on the east side of the river, some maneuvering was necessary to depart. Lewis wrote: "sent Drewyer and R. Fields with the horses to the lower side of Medecine river, and proceeded myself with all our baggage and J. Fields down the missouri to the mouth of Medecine river in our canoe of buffaloe skins. we were compelled to swim the horses above the whitebear island and again across the medicine river as the Missouri is of great width below the mouth of that river."

That evening, Lewis camped under a shelving rock just below the great falls. He had stopped there to make one last sketch (this sketch has never been found) of the falls of the Missouri. He noted, "these falls have abated much of their grandure since I first arrived at them in June 1805....however they are still a sublimely grand object."

The next morning, July 17, Lewis headed northwest. About 5 p.m., they came to the Teton River where they saw a wounded buffalo. Lewis assumed the animal had been shot by Indians and he was immediately concerned about a possible surprise meeting with them. Drouillard was dispatched in haste to finish off the buffalo and determine if indeed it had been wounded by Indians. The buffalo slipped away, but it served a warning to Lewis who demanded a strict guard be kept at night. The Captain wrote that he took his turn at night guarding the camp, just like the other men.

During the day of July 18 as the party worked its way toward the Marias River, they saw innumerable numbers of buffalo. At one point, Lewis estimated there was no break in the brown blanket for twelve miles. Ironically in just a few days, the party of four would have to shoot pigeons to ward off the hunger pains.

After crossing the Teton River and reaching the Marias, the party followed that stream to the point where the Two Medicine River and Cut Bank Creek join to form the Marias. On July 21, Lewis wrote about the decision he made at this junction. Referring to Cut Bank Creek, he noted, "being convinced that this stream came from the mountains I determined to pursue it as it will lead me to the most nothern point...which I now fear will not be as far north [50 degrees N] as I wished and expected."

Lewis proceeded up Cut Bank Creek for two days. From a bluff just south of the creek, he confirmed his concerns about the direction it was taking. He could see it headed for the distant mountains in the west. He wrote, "I thought it unnecessary to proceed further and therefore encamped resolving to rest ourselves and horses a couple of days at this place and take the necessary observations."

Lewis's Route and Campsites -
White Bear Islands to Camp Disappointment
and return to the Mouth of the Marias
1806

Glacier National Park

Continental Divide

Camp Disappointment

Cut Bank

22 July
Cut Bank ⊙
Cut Bank Creek

⊙ Browning

Two Medicine River

Badger Creek

fight site

Birch Creek

"Bactic River"

Valier ⊙

Conrad ⊙

27 July

Marias

21 July

Shelby ⊙

20 July

19 July

⊙ Chester

cache

Fort Benton ⊙

River

Missouri

"Tansy or Rose River"

Teton River

⊙ Choteau

Sun River

"Medicine River"

18 July

27/28 July

17 July

Great Falls of the Missouri

Great Falls ⊙

White Bear Islands Camp

Route
---- by land
〜〜 by water

● campsite

Lewis and his party spent four miserable days at the place he later called Camp Disappointment. The weather was cold and rainy, and clouds effectively blocked Lewis' attempt to obtain the necessary data to determine longitude of the site. Not only was the weather miserable, but efforts to secure food in the neighborhood proved fruitless. Fortunately on July 24, a flock of passenger pigeons arrived, and the men were able to shoot enough for the day's meals. The next day, they fared better as "R. Fields and myself killed nine pige[ons] which lit in the trees near our camp on these we dined." Later in the day, a fine buck deer was killed, and Lewis wrote "we now fared sumptuously."

On the 25th, Lewis finally determined to leave. He wrote, "I now begin to be apprehensive that I shall not reach the United States within this season unless I make every exertion in my power which I shall certainly not omit when once I leave this place...." The next morning, the weather was again uncooperative. Lewis left without the readings he so wanted.

INDIANS ON THE TWO MEDICINE

Following a southeast course, the party forded Badger Creek about noon on the 26th. After dining and continuing three miles farther downstream, they ascended to the plain and saw at a distance of one mile an "assembleage of about 30 horses...." Looking through his "spye glass" Lewis determined there were eight Indians and thirty horses. He wrote, "this was a very unpleasant sight, however I resolved to make the best of our situation and to approach them in a friendly manner."

Lewis' assessment of the situation was "that these were the Minnetares of Fort de Prarie and from their known character I expected that we were to have some difficulty with them; that if they thought themselves sufficiently strong I was convinced they would attempt to rob us in which case be their numbers what they would I should resist to the last extremity prefering death to that of being deprived of my papers instruments and gun and desired that they would form the same resolution and be allert and on their guard." The two parties met, dismounted and shook hands. Lewis presented gifts to three who claimed to be chiefs. He learned these warriors were part of a larger party camped to the west and that these people did trade with the British in Saskatchewan. Lewis told them about the rest of his party which was descending the Missouri River. He offered to give these men the ten horses and some tobacco if they would accompany him to the mouth of the Marias.

Camp that evening was made with the Indians near one of three solitary cottonwood trees on the Two Medicine River. Lewis wrote: "I took the first watch tonight and set up untill half after eleven; the indians by this time were all asleep, I roused up R. Fields and laid down myself; I directed Fields to watch the movements of the indians and if any of them left the camp to awake us all as I apprehended they would attampt to s[t]eal our horses. this being done I fell into a profound sleep...."

In the early morning light of July 27 with Lewis still asleep, one of the Indians took the Field brothers' guns. The Indian began to run from camp just as Joseph Field discovered what had happened. The two brothers pursued the Indian whom "they overtook at the distance of 50 or 60 paces...and R Fields as he seized his gun stabed the indian to the heart with his knife the fellow ran about 15 steps and fell dead...."

Back in camp, Lewis was awakened by Drouillard's, "damn you let go my gun...." While Drouillard wrestled for his gun, Lewis discovered his own gun was being taken by another Indian. Lewis, in pursuit of the Indian who had taken his gun, met the two Field brothers who were just returning to camp. The men wanted to kill the Indian, but Lewis forbid them "as the indian did not appear to wish to kill us...." Lewis soon changed his mind when the Indians began to drive off the horses. Lewis wrote, "I now hollowed to the men and told them to fire on them if they attempted to drive off our horses...."

Lewis pursued the Indian who had stolen his gun and was now trying to take the horses. The Indian dropped the gun which Lewis immediately picked up. He wrote: "I called to them as I had done several times before that I would shoot them if they did not give me my horse and raised my gun, one of them jumped behind a rock and spoke to the other who turned arround and stoped at the distance of 30 steps from me and I shot him through the belly, he fell to his knees and on his wright elbow from which position he partly raised himself up and fired

at me, and turning himself about crawled in behind a rock which was a few feet from him. he overshot me, being bearheaded I felt the wind of his bullet very distinctly."

Lewis did not have his shot pouch along so he was unable to reload. He returned to camp and prepared to leave. They took four of the best Indian horses and left one of theirs. Lewis burned the shields and bows and arrows left by the Indians. He noted, "I also retook the flagg but left the medal about the neck of the dead man that they might be informed who we were." They also took one of the Indian guns and some of the buffalo meat.

Lewis and his three men left the camp on the Two Medicine River and headed east of southeast toward the mouth of the Marias. His course took him away from the Marias in order to keep the hill of the Marias-Teton divide between him and any pursuers. Since Lewis had told the Indians of the party on the Missouri, he wrote, "my design was to hasten to the entrance of Maria's river as quick as possible in the hope of meeting with the canoes and party at that place having no doubt but that they would pursue us...."

Eight miles after leaving the scene they crossed Birch Creek, which Lewis named "battle river." By 3 o'clock in the afternoon they had come, by Lewis' estimation, sixty-three miles to the Teton River. Here they rested for an hour and a half to let the horses graze. Again in the saddle, they rode another seventeen miles before dark, and Lewis described the country through which they had just passed "as level as a bowling green with but little stone and few prickly pears." They stopped to kill a cow buffalo and took some meat. By moonlight, they traveled until 2 in the morning, covering what Lewis estimated to be another twenty miles. They slept here until daylight when, again, they mounted the horses and set out. The long hours spent in the saddle on the previous day and night had taken their toll on the men, and Lewis wrote, "I could scarcely stand, and the men complained of being in a similar situation however I encouraged them by telling them that our own lives as well as those of our friends and fellow travellers depended on our exertions at this moment." The men proposed that they cross the Missouri at Grog Spring. Lewis disagreed because he felt it would cost an extra day and he did not want the Indians to get to the mouth of the Marias before he did.

RENDEZVOUS ON THE MISSOURI

On July 28, 1806, Sergeant Ordway wrote in his journal, "two hunters went on eairly a head. Howard killed two deer. we proceeded on as usal about 9 A.M. we discovered on a high bank a head Capt Lewis & the three men...comming towards us on N. Side we came too Shore and fired the Swivell to Salute him & party we Saluted them also with Small arms and were rejoiced to See them &c. Capt Lewis took us all by the hand..." Lewis described his feelings of seeing his fellow travelers floating down the Missouri as one of "unspeakable satisfaction." According to Lewis, the site of this joyous, unexpected celebration took place about five miles south of Grog Spring and just north of Fort Benton. Lewis was pleased with the performance of his Indian horse and found "little reason to complain about the robery."

The horses were stripped of their baggage, turned loose on the plain and the saddles were dumped into the river. In short time, the party was back on the Missouri headed for the mouth of the

Marias. Just after noon, they arrived there and immediately began to uncover the caches. About 1 p.m., good fortune was again with the Expedition as Gass and Willard joined them on horseback. They had brought the horses down from the falls to make hunting easier during the expected wait for Lewis.

The red pirogue had rotted so much over the winter it could not be used. They removed some nails and iron from her and left her on the island at the mouth of the Marias. Amid a rain and hailstorm, the Expedition departed the area and proceeded down the Missouri River for fifteen miles where they camped under a vigilant guard.

TO ST. LOUIS

Lewis' party made excellent time, some days covering eighty miles or so, and reached the mouth of the Yellowstone River on August 7. Here the Missouri River travelers found a note from Clark indicating that due to the troublesome mosquitoes and the scarcity of game, he and his party had moved further downstream. Five days later, some fifty miles east of the border of Montana and North Dakota, Lewis overtook Clark. At the meeting, Captain Clark was alarmed by the condition of his fellow leader who had been shot accidentally by Cruzatte on August 11. Lewis and the one-eyed Cruzatte had gone into some thick brush to hunt elk when Cruzatte mistook Lewis, who was dressed in leathers, for an elk. The ball from Cruzatte's gun had passed through the flesh of Lewis' buttocks causing him extreme pain and constraining him to lie on his stomach while traveling in the white pirogue. Unable to walk, Lewis was disappointed that he had to by pass the opportunity to get a latitude of the Crow Hills in McKenzie County, North Dakota. Lewis believed this to be the most northern point of the Missouri River and had planned to take an observation there.

The Expedition proceeded on to Fort Mandan and finally arrived in St. Louis in late September. Here they learned that most people had given up hope of ever again seeing them alive.

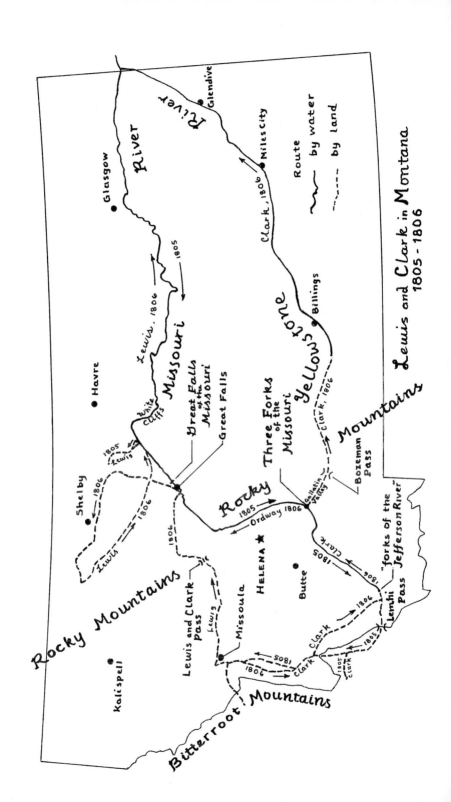

Lewis and Clark in Montana
1805 - 1806

EXPEDITION MEMBERS WHO DEPARTED FORT MANDAN

Captain Meriwether Lewis

Captain William Clark

Sergeant John Ordway

Sergeant Nathaniel Pryor

Sergeant Patrick Gass

Private William Bratton

Private John Colter

Private John Collins

Private Peter Cruzatte

Private Robert Frazier

Private Joseph Field

Private Reuben Field

Private George Gibson

Private Silas Goodrich

Private Hugh Hall

Private Thomas Howard

Private Hugh McNeal

Private John Potts

Private George Shannon

Private John Shields

Private John Thompson

Private William Werner

Private Alexander Willard

Private Richard Windsor

Private Joseph Whitehouse

Private Peter Weiser

Private John Baptiste Lepage

Interpreter George Drouillard

Interpreter Toussaint Charbonneau

Sacagawea

Jean Baptiste Charbonneau

Private Francois Labiche
York, Clark's servant
Seaman, Lewis' dog

Sergeant Charles Floyd, member of the permanent party, died August 20, 1804 near the present-day city of Sioux City, Iowa.

INDEX

REFERENCES

Allen, John L. *Passages Through the Garden: Lewis and Clark and the Images of the American Northwest.* Urbana: University of Illinois Press, 1975.

Anderson, Irving W. "Probing the Riddle of the Bird Woman," *Montana, the Magazine of Western History* 23 (1973): 2-17.

Biddle, Nicholas, editor. *The Journals of the Expedition Under Command of Captains Lewis and Clark,* Volumes 1, 2. New York: The Heritage Press, 1962.

Boorstin, Daniel J. *The Lost World of Thomas Jefferson.* Boston: Beacon Press, Third Printing, October, 1964.

Burroughs, Raymond Darwin. *The Natural History of the Lewis and Clark Expedition.* Michigan State University Press, 1961.

Chuinard, Eldon G. *Only One Man Died: The Medical Aspects of the Lewis and Clark Expedition.* Glendale, CA.: Arthur H. Clarke, 1979.

Clark, Ella E., and Margot Edmonds. *Sacagawea of the Lewis and Clark Expedition.* Berkely: University of California Press, 1979.

Clarke, Charles G. *The Men of the Lewis and Clark Expedition: A Biographical Roster of the Fifty-one Members and a Composite Dairy of Their Activities from all Known Sources.* Glendale, CA.: Arthur H. Clarke, 1970.

Cutright, Paul Russell. *Lewis and Clark Pioneering Naturalists.* Urbana: University of Illinois Press, 1969.

Cutright, Paul Russell. *A History of the Lewis and Clark Journals.* Norman: University of Oklahoma Press, 1976.

De Conde, Alexander. *This Affair of Lousiana.* New York: Charles Scribner's Sons, 1976.

Dye, Eva Emery. *Conquest the True Story of Lewis and Clark.* Binfords and Mort, 1936.

Furtwangler, Albert. *Acts of Discovery.* Urbana: University of Illinois Press, 1993.

Gass, Patrick. *A Journal of the Voyages and Travels of a Corps of Discovery.* Minneapolis: Ross&Haines, Inc., 1958.

Great Falls Tribune. Great Falls, Montana, February 6, 1886; April 14, 15, 16, 1897.

Hebard, Grace Raymond. *Sacajawea.* Glendale, CA.: Arthur H. Clark Co., 1957.

Jackson, Donald, ed. *Letters of the Lewis and Clark Expedition with Related Documents,* 1783-1854, 2nd ed., 2 vols. Urbana: University of Illinois Press, 1978.

Jackson, Donald. *Among the Sleeping Giants.* Urbana: University of Illinois Press, 1987.

Jackson, Donald. *Thomas Jefferson and The Stony Mountains.* Urbana: University of Illinois Press, 1981.

Maclean, Norman. *Young Men and Fire.* Chicago: The University of Chicago Press, 1992

Martin, Edward T. *Thomas Jefferson: Scientist.* New York: Henry Schuman, 1952.

Moulton, Gary E., ed. *The Journals of the Lewis and Clark Expedition,* 12 volumes. Lincoln: University of Nebraska Press.

Osgood, Ernest Staples. "Our Dog Scannon–Partner in Discovery," *We Proceeded On,* July 1977.

Quaife, Milo Milton, ed. *The Journals of Captain Meriwether Lewis and Sergeant John Ordway of the Expedition of Western Exploration,* 1803-1806. Madison: State Historical Society of Wisconsin, 1916.

Ronda, James P. *Lewis and Clark Among the Indians.* Lincoln: University of Nebraska Press, 1984.

Thwaites, Reuben Gold, ed. *Original Journals of the Lewis and Clark Expedition,* 1804-1806. 8 vols. New York: Arno Press, 1969.

Walcheck, Kenneth. *The Lewis and Clark Expedition: Montana's First Bird Inventory Through the Eyes of Lewis and Clark.* Great Falls, Montana: Lewis and Clark Interpretative Association, 1999.

ABOUT THE LEWIS AND CLARK INTERPRETATIVE ASSOCIATION, INC.

The Lewis and Clark Interpretative Association seeks to preserve the integrity of the Lewis and Clark Expedition by providing individuals and groups with historical and scientific information about the Expedition. It looks for opportunities to obtain materials that explain and interpret facts of the Expedition, particularly the portion that took place in Montana and the upper Missouri River. With these materials, the Association disseminates information about the Expedition by encouraging educational activities and stimulating scientific investigation and research. The association also operates and manages the commercial sale of educational items that pertain to the Expedition to stimulate interest in this important historical period.

This book is an exceptional work on Lewis and Clark in central Montana. It is a classic mixture of eloquent descriptive writing, historical anecdote and natural history.

—Terry Korpela, Lewis and Clark Interpretative Association, Inc.

The Portage Cache Gift Shop is located in The Lewis and Clark Interpretative Center in Great Falls, Montana or can be accessed through the website/corpsofdiscovery.org